Arrows in the Gale
& Other Poems

Arturo Giovannitti

Quale Press

Afterword & Chronology copyright © 2004 by Gian Lombardo. Many thanks to Robert D'Attilio for biographical information on Arturo Giovannitti.

Front Cover: Martial Law in New England, Lawrence Mill Strike, 1912; courtesy of the Industrial Workers of the World

Back Cover: Cartoon by C.R. Smith published in the *Industrial Worker,* August 15, 1912; courtesy of the Industrial Workers of the World

ISBN: 0-9700663-9-2

LCCN: 2003096114

Quale Press
www.quale.com

Contents

Arrows in the Gale

Ex Voto

Hail, full of grace, with Thee my love abides!
For thy faith which in me doth live and rest,
Blest be thy name forevermore and blest
Be Thou amongst the maidens and the brides.

Athwart the chasm that hope and fear divides
Twas Thou, the dream unseen, that I caressed,
Farther than Thee I have no goal to quest
But what thy will for thine own joy provides.

Bid me, then, gather in thy whispered name,
As in a conjured charm, all my war cries
And slay the monster that our pinions grips.

Nobler than on my brow the wreath of fame,
Holier than heaven's radiance in mine eyes
Is thy young kiss of love upon my lips.

Proem

These are but songs — they're not a creed
    They are not meant to lift or save,
They won't appeal or intercede
    For any fool or any knave;
They hold no covenant or pledge
    For him who dares no foe assail:
They are the blows of my own sledge
    Against the walls of my own jail.

I stand a watch at the van post
    Of my own war I'm captain of;
No holy fire of Pentecost
    Can force on me a Saviour's love.
I fight alone and win or sink,
    I need no one to make me free,
I want no Jesus Christ to think
    That he could ever die for me.

If what I have I give, you can
        Be sure I lay no heavenly store,
And what I take from any man
        I have no thankful feeling for.
All that you worship, fear and trust
        I kick into the sewer's maw
And fling my shaft and my disgust
        Against your gospel and your law.

Oh, yes, I know the firing line
        Outstretches far beyond my arms,
I know this muffled song of mine
        Is but one shout of many alarms;
But though along the battle range
        I press with many in one pursuit,
I have my personal revenge,
        My private enemy to shoot.

To them, the hosts of every land,
        The nameless army of the strong
Who make Humanity's last stand
        Against the battlements of wrong,
No worthy anthem can attune
        My raucous *buccina*. Let him,
The greater bard that shall come soon,
        Sing through the cannon mouth their hymn.

To them, for theirs and for my sake,
        He'll speak the words I never spoke,
And if he speak them, let him take
        The laurel wreath, the crown of oak.
For what they win is theirs alone,
        Of their reward I ask no part,
I only claim three things my own:
        My dream, my death and my sweetheart.

But if they want my song — 'tis theirs.
        For though it may not stir their souls,
Though feebler than their bugle blares,
        Their drum taps and their tocsin tolls,

Still may my song, before the sun's
    Reveille, speed the hours that tire,
While they are cleaning up their guns
    Around the cheery bivouac fire.

THE PRISONER'S BENCH

Through here all wrecks of the tempestous mains
    Of life have washed away the tides of time.
Tatters of flesh and souls, furies and pains,
    Horrors and passions awful or sublime,
All passed here to their doom. Nothing remains
    Of all the tasteless dregs of sin and crime
But stains of tears, and stains of blood and stains
    Of the inn's vomit and the brothel's grime.

And now we, too, must sit here, Joe. Don't dust
These boards on which our wretched brothers fell,
They are clean, there's no reason for disgust.
For the fat millionaire's revolting stench
Is not here, nor the preacher's saintly smell,
And the judge never sat upon this bench.

THE WALKER

I hear footsteps over my head all night.

They come and they go. Again they come and they go all night.

They come one eternity in four paces and they go one eternity in four paces, and between the coming and the going there is Silence and the Night and the Infinite.

For infinite are the nine feet of a prison cell, and endless is the march of him who walks between the yellow brick wall and the red iron gate, thinking things that cannot be chained and cannot be locked, but that wander far away in the sunlit world, each in a wild pilgrimage after a destined goal.

* * *

5

Throughout the restless night I hear the footsteps over my head.

Who walks? I know not. It is the phantom of the jail, the sleepless brain, a man, the man, the Walker.

One-two-thee-four: four paces and the wall.

One-two-three-four: four paces and the iron gate.

He has measured his space, he has measured it accurately, scrupulously, minutely, as the hangman measures the rope and the gravedigger the coffin — so many feet, so many inches, so many fractions of an inch for each of the four paces.

One-two-three-four. Each step sounds heavy and hollow over my head, and the echo of each step sounds hollow within my head as I count them in suspense and in dread that once, perhaps, in the endless walk, there may be five steps instead of four between the yellow brick wall and the red iron gate.

But he has measured the space so accurately, so scrupulously, so minutely that nothing breaks the grave rhythm of the slow, fantastic march.

* * *

When all are asleep (and who knows but I when all sleep?) three things are still awake in the night: the Walker, my heart and the old clock which has the soul of a fiend — for never, since a coarse hand with red hair on its fingers swung for the first time the pendulum in the jail, has the old clock tick-tocked a full hour of joy.

Yet the old clock which marks everything, and records everything, and to everything tolls the death knell, the wise old clock that knows everything, does not know the number of the footsteps of the Walker, nor the throbs of my heart.

For not for the Walker, nor for my heart is there a second, a minute, an hour or anything that is in the old clock — there is nothing but the night, the sleepless night, the watchful, wistful night, and footsteps that go, and footsteps that come and the wild, tumultuous beatings that trail after them forever.

* * *

All the sounds of the living beings and inanimate things, and all the voices and all the noises of the night I have heard in my wistful vigil.

I have heard the moans of him who bewails a thing that is dead and the sighs of him who tries to smother a thing that will not die;

I have heard the stifled sobs of the one who weeps with his head under the coarse blankets, and the whisperings of the one who prays with his forehead on the hard, cold stone of the floor;

I have heard him who laughs the shrill, sinister laugh of folly at the horror rampant on the yellow wall and at the red eyes of the nightmare glaring through the iron bars;

I have heard in the sudden icy silence him who coughs a dry, ringing cough, and wished madly that his throat would not rattle so and that he would not spit on the floor, for no sound was more atrocious than that of his sputum upon the floor;

I have heard him who swears fearsome oaths which I listen to in reverance and awe, for they are
   holier than the virgin's prayer;
And I have heard, most terrible of all, the silence of two hundred brains all possessed by one sin-
   gle, relentless, unforgiving, desperate thought.
All this have I heard in the watchful night,
   And the murmur of the wind beyond the walls,
   And the tolls of a distant bell,
   And the woeful dirge of the rain,
And the remotest echoes of the sorrowful city
And the terrible beatings, wild beatings, mad beatings of the One Heart which is nearest to my
   heart.
All this have I heard in the still night;
But nothing is louder, harder, drearier, mightier, more awful than the footsteps I hear over my
   head all night.

* * *

Yet fearsome and terrible are all the footsteps of men upon the earth, for they either descend or
   climb.
They descend from little mounds and high peaks and lofty altitudes, through wide roads and
   narrow paths, down noble marble stairs and creaky stairs of wood — and some go down
   to the cellar, and some to the grave, and some down to the pits of shame and infamy, and
   still some to the glory of an unfathomable abyss where there is nothing but the staring
   white, stony eyeballs of Destiny.
And again other footsteps climb. They climb to life and to love, to fame, to power, to vanity, to
   truth, to glory and to the scaffold — to everything but Freedom and the Ideal.
And they all climb the same roads and the same stairs others go down; for never, since man
   began to think how to overcome and overpass man, have other roads and other stairs been
   found.
They descend and they climb, the fearful footsteps of men, and some limp, some drag, some
   speed, some trot, some run — they are quiet, slow, noisy, brisk, quick, feverish, mad, and
   most awful is their cadence to the ears of the one who stands still.
But of all the footsteps of men that either descend or climb, no footsteps are so fearsome and
   terrible as those that go straight on the dead level of a prison floor, from a yellow stone
   wall to a red iron gate.

* * *

All through the night he walks and he thinks. Is it more frightful because he walks and his foot-
   steps sound hollow over my head, or because he thinks and speaks not his thoughts?
But does he think? Why should he think? Do I think? I only hear the footsteps and count them.
   Four steps and the wall. Four steps and the gate. But beyond? Beyond? Where goes he
   beyond the gate and the wall?

He goes not beyond. His thought breaks there on the iron gate. Perhaps it breaks like a wave of rage, perhaps like a sudden flow of hope, but it always returns to beat the wall like a billow of helplessness and despair.

He walks to and fro within the narrow whirlpit of this ever storming and furious thought. Only one thought — constant, fixed, immovable, sinister, without power and without voice.

A thought of madness, frenzy, agony and despair, a hell-brewed thought, for it is a natural thought. All things natural are things impossible while there are jails in the world — bread, work, happiness, peace, love.

But he thinks not of this. As he walks he thinks of the most superhuman, the most unattainable, the most impossible thing in the world:

He thinks of a small brass key that turns just half around and throws open the red iron gate.

* * *

That is all the Walker thinks, as he walks throughout the night.

And that is what two hundred minds drowned in the darkness and the silence of the night think, and that is also what I think.

Wonderful is the supreme wisdom of the jail that makes all think the same thought. Marvelous is the providence of the law that equalizies all, even in mind and sentiment. Fallen is the last barrier of privilege, the aristocracy of the intellect. The democracy of reason has leveled all the two hundred minds to the common surface of the same thought.

I, who have never killed, think like the murderer;

I, who have never stolen, reason like the thief;

I think, reason, wish, hope, doubt, wait like the hired assassin, the embezzler, the forger, the counterfeiter, the incestuous, the raper, the drunkard, the prostitute, the pimp, I, I who used to think of love and life and flowers and song and beauty and the ideal.

A little key, a little key as little as my little finger, a little key of shining brass.

All my ideas, my thoughts, my dreams are congealed in a little key of shiny brass.

All my brain, all my soul, all the suddenly surging latent powers of my deepest life are in the pocket of a white-haired man dressed in blue.

He is great, powerful, formidable, the man with the white hair, for he has in his pocket the mighty talisman which makes one man cry, and one man pray, and one laugh, and one cough, and one walk, and all keep awake and listen and think the same maddening thought.

Greater than all men is the man with the white hair and the small brass key, for no other man in the world could compel two hundred men to think for so long the same thought. Surely when the light breaks I will write a hymn unto him which shall hail him greater than Mohammed and Arbues and Torquemada and Mesmer, and all the other masters of other men's thoughts. I shall call him Almighty, for he holds everything of all and of me in a little brass key in his pocket.

Everything of me he holds but the branding iron of contempt and the claymore of hatred for the monstrous cabala that can make the apostle and the murderer, the poet and the procurer, think of the same gate, the same key and the same exit on the different sunlit highways of life.

* * *

My brother, do not walk any more.

It is wrong to walk on a grave. It is a sacrilege to walk four steps from the headstone to the foot and four steps from the foot to the headstone.

If you stop walking, my brother, no longer will this be a grave, for you will give me back my mind that is chained to your feet and the right to think my own thoughts.

I implore you, my brother, for I am weary of the long vigil, weary of counting your steps, and heavy with sleep.

Stop, rest, sleep, my brother, for the dawn is well nigh and it is not the key alone that can throw open the gate.

THE THINKER — ON RODIN'S STATUE

Aye, think! Since time and life began,
    Your mind has only feared and slept;
Of all the beasts they called you man
    Only because you toiled and wept.

On all the ages firmly set,
    Lone pillar of the world you stood;
Beyond your hunger and your sweat
    You never knew, nor understood —

Till now, when deep into your soul,
    Where it lay buried and concealed,
At last your destined end and goal
    Shall stand emblazoned and revealed.

Think, think — unburden, liberate
    Your mind from all its waste and loss,
Throw down from it the age-long weight
    Of few men's feet and one man's cross.

Behind your mighty frame, in fright
    To stay you, moan the dark, dead years.

Heed not the voices of the night,
    Heed not the echoes of your tears.

However dear, your sorrows rest
    Upon you, like a burial stone.
Upturn it! Rise! Their grave's unblest,
    The terrors of the past have flown.

Its memories in you must die,
    Its shadows must depart from you,
Your doubts, your fears are all a lie,
    Only this wondrous thought is true.

Think! If your brain will but extend
    As far as what your hands have done,
If but your reason will descend
    As deep as where your feet have gone —

The walls of ignorance will fall
    That stood between you and your world,
And from its bloody pedestal
    The last god, Terror, shall be hurled.

Aye, think! While breaks in you the dawn,
    Crouched at your feet, the world lies still —
It has no power but your brawn,
    It knows no wisdom but your will.

Behind your flesh, and mind and blood
    Nothing there is to live and do,
There is no man, there is no god,
    There is not anything but you.

Think, think! What every age and land
    Thought an eternal mystery,
What seers could never understand
    And saints and sages could not see,

From you, the chained, reviled outcast,
    From you the brute inert and dumb,
Shall, through your wakened thought at last,
    The message of to-morrow come.

It will come like a shaft of light,
        A truth to love and to redeem,
    And — whether Love or Dynamite —
        Shall lead the pathway to your dream.

THE STRANGER AT THE GATE

The Stranger whose sandals were white with the dust of many roads approached the guardian
    of the gate on his way out of the mighty city, whose towers are loftier than the pillars of
    smoke and the mountain peaks in the sky,
"Peace and plenty be with thee forever, keeper of the gate," said he, touching with two fingers
    of his right hand his bowed forehead.
"God walk before thy feet forevermore, stranger," answered the keeper of the gate.
    "Whither goest thou?"
"Wherever men are and the highroads lead. For the wisdom I seek does not remain in one place.
    It beckons and I follow, keeper of the gate."
"Hast thou found any wisdom in our city, stranger?"
"Aye, much wisdom have I found and great knowledge for the wayfarer who seeks a home to
    rest in his old age. My home is farther on the road, keeper of the gate."
"Who told thee that thy home is not in our city, stranger?"
"The man ye crucified yesterday. He cried not, nor did he weep nor curse as such men do, but
    he smiled and he smiled and he looked at me strangely, oh, so strangely!"
"And what said he that thou leavest a great city because of the words of a criminal?"
"Nay, he said naught, but I said unto myself, instead, that the city where crucified wrongdoers
    cry not, nor weep, nor curse, but smile and look so strangely at people, is no place for the
    stranger who has seen many lands and knows many roads, keeper of the gate."
"He smiled to hurt and infuriate us, stranger, for we are used to shrieks and curses. He was the
    worst offender of all, as thou mayest judge by his ungodly behavior. Not even death
    appeased or terrified him."
"Aye, so methought, in sooth. But prithee, keeper of the gate, why did ye crucify him?"
"Knowest thou not the laws of this land which is the wealthiest and mightiest under the sun?
    He deserved death."
"Aye, any dead man deserved death, but I know not for what reason."
"He did offend against the sovereignty of the people and the godliness of our supreme law,
    stranger."
"Verily, it is so, keeper of the gate. But was it, perchance, because, as I heard, he pitied the poor
    and the lowly?"
"Nay, 'twas not for that. We also pity them. Indeed we have many great institutions that shel-
    ter the worthy poor."

"Was it, then, because he mingled with the rabble and flattered it with strange and obscure words such as right, justice and the like?"

"Not for that, indeed, for we do the same. How else could we get the recruits for the legions, the votes to elect the Sanhedrim and the populace to cheer the Tetrarch and the Proconsul?"

"In faith, then it was because he believed in a new religion, contrary to the established church?"

"Say not that again, stranger, or I shall think that thou hast not gathered much knowledge in thy many journeys. Thou shouldst know, forsooth, that we are very tolerant in religious matters and that our Pantheon hath a niche for every god. The more religions we have the better, so says the Praetor."

"Upon my head, thou hast spoken the truth, keeper of the gate. Then I gather that it was because he forgave the adulterous woman."

"Not so, stranger. We had good divorce laws ere he came, and many unmarried men in the land who would rather wed a repudiated woman than a maiden."

"By my rod, so it is, keeper of the gate. So I infer that it was because he pardoned the harlot of yonder city I passed last week."

"Nay, nay, thou speakest not wisely, stranger. Harlotry is a necessary evil, as many wise men have often declared, but thou hast surely heard of late that we have appointed councils of rich and powerful men to abate it and redeem the fallen women."

"Indeed, I heard of it and it is a most worthy and honorable enterprise, keeper of the gate. But now I know it truly: it was, no doubt, because he said that these rich men could not enter the kingdoms of the blessed hereafter."

"Nay, not for that, stranger. Everybody says that, even the high priests of the temples. It is by saying that, that the rich men are kept on this earth, as I heard a Pharisee tell a wealthy publican."

"Then my knowledge goes not farther, keeper of the gate. I beg of thee to tell me outright why ye crucified him, if thou wouldst teach a poor wayfarer who is seeking after wisdom."

"Aye, I will tell thee, stranger, though thy curiosity is great for a walker of Caesar's roads. It was not because of any of these things, but because of all these things, because he said and did them all at once and because he talked too much and was beginning to be heard and because . . . But whither art thou going, stranger?"

"Where the highroad leads, keeper of the gate."

TO A BENCH IN MULBERRY PARK

Well, after many a year,
I see thou art still here,
Old bench, old haven of my roaming days;
And like a canopy

On royal beds, on thee
Its green pavilion still the maple sprays.

They were not sweet, indeed,
Those dreary days of need
When I, each night, would wonder here alone
Whether the dawn would hail
Another thief in jail
Or at the morgue another corpse unknown.

They were, indeed, so crude,
Those days of solitude,
When hunger grinned at madness' stony stare —
Recall not that again,
For love has come since then
And youth has won the battle with despair.

Those songs instead evoke
That sobs and tears did choke,
And that young faith no tempest could destroy;
Recall the tunes I knew,
The dreams each morning slew,
And those that since fulfilled their task of joy.

When every roar and sound
The heartless city drowned
Into the surging ocean of the night,
To me alone would drift,
A rich and kingly gift,
The flotsam of its song for my delight.

From all these windows purred
The slumbers, and I heard,
Now and again, a cradling mother croon,
While from the roofs afar
Dropped from an old guitar
The sighs of some young lover to the moon.

Watching the clouds' odd race
In my ecstatic maze
Meseemed that thou into their sea didst soar,
And I went sailing by,

Young Orpheus of the sky,
Like a doge in a gorgeous bucentaur.

I dreamed and dreamed all night,
Young dreams, and frail and bright,
Like little buds that never grow to bloom,
Like silver clouds that pass,
Like crickets in the grass,
Like yellow fireflies twinkling in the gloom.

Yea, I was hungry — yet
Sometimes one can forget
And hungry stomachs often find a dole,
But the young days are fleet
When one can fill with sweet
And moonlit dreams the hunger of the soul.

Ah me! they're gone, those days,
And love for me now lays
A pillow full of lullabies to sleep;
But it is hard, alack!
That memories come back
Of days that were so sad when one can't weep.

Yet in my deepest heart
I feel a sudden smart
That I won't tell my love and she won't see —
Old bench, if some new wretch
His limbs on thee should stretch,
Be kind to him as thou hast been to me.

OUT OF THE MOUTHS OF BABES

Milady was sitting at the table under the pink wax-light, alone in the resplendent hall.
I looked in from the street and knew not what resplended the most, whether the young, blue-
clad sweetness of milady or the chaste sheen of the tablecloth, or the luster of the cande-
labra, the silver, the gold, the crystal, or, mayhap, the lucid head of the severe and solemn
waiter.

But I knew that the waiter was there because of milady and not milady because of the waiter, as some may think.

Milady was there only because of the little, fragile shivering bitch she held in her arms, and the little bitch had her little paws on the white tablecloth while milady fed to her, delicately and amorously the soul and the brain of the waiter diluted with a little spoon of gold in a creamy fluid, in a noble silver bowl.

Alone milady sat in the great hall under the pink wax-light as I watched her through the frost-embroidered window, and methought she was Hebe ministering the nectar to the last god.

Outside, the great black carriage awaited under the nimble-limbed portico of alabaster, and the little newsboy who stood by me devoured with his eyes, perhaps the uncarnal beauty of milady, perhaps the heavenly gruel of the shivering bitch.

I looked at him and deeply I looked into his ravenous eyes, and then I asked: "Of what are you thinking, my little friend?"

Said he: "I have sold six papers in four hours and the papers are now wet and old, for they age and die in few hours, the papers."

Said he: "My mother is dead, my father is in jail, my sister is in the saloon and I have sold only six papers in four hours."

Said he again: "I wish I was that dog."

Again I looked at him, and his eyes were full of tears, the child tears that only the women understand, the young tears that make men smile.

And I said: "Yea, boy, for if you were that dog you would be sure to eat and to be petted to-night.

"And also, if you can kiss no more your mother, at least you could lap the hand of your mistress, for she is very dear and very sweet. Is it not so?"

He raised his eyes to me, his big blue eyes, his placid eyes full of tears and he glared at me and answered through his clenched teeth:

"No, damn you, no, I would tear her nose off."

And he darted away in the raging blizzard.

But I saw the sun, the sun, the great sun, the luminous warm sun, right in the front of him.

THE BUM

The dust of a thousand roads, the grease
    And grime of slums, were on his face;
The fangs of hunger and disease
    Upon his throat had left their trace,
The smell of death was in his breath,
    But in his eye no resting place.

Along the gutters, shapeless, fagged,
    With drooping head and bleeding feet,
Throughout the Christmas night he dragged
    His care, his woe, and his defeat;
Till gasping hard with face downward
    He fell upon the trafficked street.

The midnight revelry aloud
    Cried out its glut of wine and lust;
The happy, clean, indifferent crowd
    Passed him in anger and disgust;
For — fit or rum — he was a bum,
    And if he died 'twas nothing lost.

The tramp, the thief, the drunk, the brute,
    The beggar, each withdrew his eye;
E'en she, the bartered prostitute,
    Held close her skirts and passed him by;
For, drunk or dead, the street's the bed
    Where dogs and bums must sleep and die.

So all went on to their debauch,
    Parade of ghosts in weird array.
Only a tramp dog did approach
    That mass of horror and decay —
It sniffed him out with its black snout
    Then turned about and limped away.

And there he lay, a thing of dread,
    A loathsome thing for man and beast;
None put a stone beneath his head,
    Or wet his lips, or rubbed his wrist,
And none drew near to help or cheer —
    Save a policeman and a priest.

Yet neither heard his piteous wail,
    And neither knelt by where he fell.
The man in blue spoke of the jail,
    Until he heard his rattle tell,
And hearing that, he motioned at
    The man in black to speak of hell.

To speak of hell, lest he should hope
    For peace, for rest untroubled, deep,
Where he no more need roam and grope
    Through dark, foul lanes to beg and weep,
Where in the vast warm earth at last
    He'd find a resting place to sleep.

To sleep — not standing tired and sick
    By grimy walls and cold lamp poles,
Nor crouched in fear of the night stick,
    To beat his sore and swollen soles,
Nor see the flares of green nightmares
    And ghastly dawns through black rat holes;

To sleep beneath the green, warm earth
    As in a sacred mother's womb,
And wait the call of a new birth,
    When his dead life again shall bloom —
For it shall pass into the grass;
    The lamb will graze upon his tomb.

Not he, not he shall think of this,
    Not he the wretched, the down trod;
Beyond the club of the police
    Shall reach the ruthless hand of God,
For like a ghoul the rich man's rule
    Will seek him out beneath the sod.

He must know hell, lest he should guess
    That all his weary tramp is o'er —
A hell of hunger and distress
    Where he, cold, naked and footsore,
Alone and ill, must wander still
    Through endless roads forevermore.

Nay, nay, my brother, 'tis a lie!
    Just like their Christ, their love, their law!
They brewed a wolfish fiend on high,
    Just like their hearts perverse and raw,
To damn or save the dying slave,
    So those who live should serve in awe.

So that in trembling fear they'd hold
　　　Upon their neck their masters' sway,
So that they'd guard their masters' gold
　　　And starve and freeze and still obey,
So when for greed they toil and bleed,
　　　Instead of rising they should pray.

That's why they come to huts and slums!
　　　'Tis not to soothe or to console,
But just to stay the hungry bums
　　　With this black terror of the soul,
And bend and blight with chains of fright
　　　What chains of steel could not control.

And yet, and yet the thunderbolt
　　　Shall fall some day they fear the least,
When flesh and sinews shall revolt
　　　And she, the mob, the fiend, the beast,
Unchained, awake, shall turn and break
　　　The bloody tables of their feast.

But you, my brother, will be dead,
　　　And none will think of you for aye!
Still by your spirit I'll be led,
　　　If like their cattle you'll not die,
If you'll but show before you go
　　　That mine can be your battle cry!

Aye, brother, death all woes relieves —
　　　Yet this low world that well you knew,
This Christian world of sainted thieves
　　　And fat apostles of virtue,
This world of brutes and prostitutes,
　　　Must see its end revealed by you!

Rise then! Your rags, your bleeding shirt,
　　　Tear from your crushed and trampled chest,
Fling in its face its own vile dirt,
　　　Your scorn and hate to manifest,
And in its gray cold eyes of prey
　　　Spit out your life and your protest!

— Salem Jail, November 20, 1912

The Magdalene

The service over, the silk-hatted pastor,
    Smooth-shaven, jovial, fat and debonair,
A merry joke on his ascetic master,
    Met in the empty church a woman's stare.

He paused, his hands on his rotund abdomen
    Piously laid, and quoth with solemn mien
"What can I do for you, my worthy woman?"
    She rose and said: "I am the Magdalene."

"You said that I believed and was forgiven,
    That faith alone can save and purify,
And from the stews I came, whence I was driven,
    To seal upon your lips the monstrous lie.

"For though I have believed and not denied Him,
    Though with my bitter tears I washed His feet,
The harpy clutch of greed that crucified Him
    Has dragged me back into the sunless street.

"From pit to pit it dragged me down, a mourner
    Of His great shattered dream, with blows and sneers,
And you have seen me stand around the corner,
    A traded strumpet for two thousand years.

"You saw them with their hands of fiendish malice,
    From this, my withered, soulless flesh of pain,
Wring out the gold with which they bought the chalice
    Where now you gulp his precious blood again.

"All this you saw, and still to them that Jesus
    Drove from his house, aye, from this very place,
You sell his heaven for thirty silver pieces,
    And for a mess of potage my disgrace.

"You call on them his blessing while I wander
    On all the ways of hell where I was thrust,
And while you soothe their glutted souls, you pander
    To my eternal shame and to their lust.

"And yet I know, in all my desolation,
    The Saviour shall soon come to my release,
No more a doleful voice or resignation,
    No more a God-sent messenger of peace,

"But a red-winged archangel of the devil
    Who shall disperse for aye the ravenous brood,
Your lies hush in the offals of their revel,
    And give me back my soul and womanhood."

THE PRAISE OF SPRING

I have hated thee, O Spring.
With all the furies of my inextinguishable blood,
    With all the aches of my unappeasable flesh
    I have hated thee,
    And despised thee,
    And cursed thee, O Spring.
I have hated thee for the stupidity of thy flowers that smelled the carrion of the covered graves,
For the acquiescent foolishness of thy ever nodding trees,
For the frigid chastity of thy skies,
For the garrulity of thy silly cackling waters
And for the petulance of thy eternal reappearing,
O thou idiotic, unoriginal repentance of the decrepit earth.
I have hated thee because thou wert an atonement, not a rebellion; thou wert a returning child-
    hood, not a reconquered virility. O Spring.
No storms, no tempests, no hurricanes,
No spasms of long-nursed follies,
No violences of coveted passions,
No brazen display of warm desires and unclad sins,
No exaltation of fecund motherhood,
Nothing but the recurrence of an old fashion, the re-wearing of the discarded, ignoble dress of
    green, a new coat of perfumed rouge over the wrinkles of the same old yellow face of the
    world.

* * *

I have hated thee, O Spring. With all the impetuosity of my living being I have hated thee.

I have hated thee for the evil filter of thy air, that abominable potion that has nothing but the effervescence of its bubbles,

That tasteless broth of malignity which does not inebriate like a generous wine,

Which does not kill like a magnificent poison,

Which is neither a bitter medicine that heals the heart-fevers of youth, nor a sweet narcotic that gives sleep.

That wert a painted and tinseled masquerade,

O Spring, a stimulant for old age, not a cordial for battling manhood, and no life was in thee save the fermentation of dead things.

The life that grew not out of the creating labors of love, but out of the stillness of corpses, so that the warrior Winter again might have ought to destroy.

The purveyor of Death, not the handmaid of Life thou wert, for no nurslings that the grave could not claim were ever to sleep in the warmth of thy breasts.

* * *

But why, even for that and because of that, did I hate thee, O Spring?

Was it the overpowering onrush of manhood that was invading my soul and sweeping away from it the dreams, the follies, the chimeras of my silent, wide-eyed, ghost-like youth?

Was it because, in spite of thy breath, laden with all the unknowable maladies of the invisible life, my heart wounds, my soul wounds whose crusts I had been tearing with my sharp nails, were healing and no longer I loved to torment their pain?

Or was it the pale light of a vision I had kindled with the first spark of my childhood and fed with the shreds of my years, that suddenly blazed forth like a terrible pyre for the conflagration of the world thou camest back to refresh and regreen?

Whoever will know and tell? Whoever cares to know?

Not I, not I, O Spring.

I was alone, I who was alive in myself, was alone in thy dead splendor a thousandfold resurrected and a thousandfold annihilated,

And I who could be killed but once and nevermore be arisen,

I who carried the burden of but one single life, the burden I never tried to lighten but ever tried to increase with my greedy, far-reaching all-apprehending hands,

I sneered the contempt of my glorious mortality unto thee that art not immovable and eternal and yet art not forever to die.

For it is engraved on the vaults of the unassailable firmaments and it is burned in the dark of the unfathomable profundities that they alone who are to meet death are the master and the commanders of life.

* * *

21

There was I alone with my challenge against thee and thy mother, O Spring.

And thy wiles and thy lures that made thee the easy-yielding courtesan of all creatures had no power and no charm over me, the rebellious child of sin.

And for this I hated thee, because there was no chastity, in thee, because thou wert the common mistress of all and I was waiting for the Virgin-Bride of the Ideal.

And my glory grew as great as my strength, and my strength as great as my desire, because of my solitude.

There was in my beating temples the panting of the only reality of life,

All the onslaught of time was ramming and breaking against my bare and villous chest.

All the red-maned steeds of destruction, trembling with the furious lust of the race were leashed to my fist;

And I who had breathed the warm wind of the battle-field,

    And the raging soul of the storm,

    And the ashes of the galloping fire,

    And the dust of the things destroyed,

I, who shed tears only when I looked open-eyed at the noon sun,

I heard in the echo of my steps in thy woods the footfalls of the bronze-shod Vandal though the columns of the burned and pillaged temple where all the tripods blazed with the Greek fire and the face of the stone gods was ground under the ironed hoof of the stallions.

For this I hated thee, O Spring, because I was a destroyer and not a worshipper of silent things.

And because I was waiting for the scarlet-robed, flame-winged, storm-haired Bride of the Future for whose nuptials a greater altar fire shall be built than that of the volcanoes,

I flung into the face of that old mother of yours, Nature, whose obscene nakedness, polluted by the vile caresses of all the distorted fingers of greed thou wert recovering with thy tawdry mantle of green, not my staff, O Spring, not my javelin, not my broken spur, but just one word, just one word, O Spring.

II

And now thou hast returned again.

Again thou hast returned with thy green and thy blue and thy gold and thy breezes, but lo! thou art so strangely and so wildly different unto my eyes and into the mirror where my eyes cannot look, O Spring.

For the day I saw the first dandelion and the first daisy and I heard the first strident voice of the cricket, the little messengers that announced thee, that day I was alone no more.

Another one was by my side, and she was young, and she was fair, and she was lost like me in the gateless labyrinth of life.

Like me she had nursed her youth with the divine nectar of the tempests,

Like me she was cruel with many angers and sad with many cares,

Like me she understood the lofty virtues of hatred and the endless march onward to the gate that does not exist, with no other compass to guide our feet but our will to go.

Yet was she not like me, for on her forehead there were not the scars of the fierce affrays,
On her lips there were not the bitter wrinkles furrowed by the long, unerasable sneers,
Nor on her wrists the marks of torn and broken fetters and chains,
Nor the shadows of crossed darknesses had remained in her limpid eyes.
She was not like me, yet much that was in me was in her, and because her destiny, like mine,
compelled her to go and never to look behind, I paused with her and in her I forgot all thy
malevolence and all my hatred of thee, O Spring.
And there were two alive in the old world-cemetery of corpses, she and I in the immense crypt
of the universe, O Spring.

* * *

Why dost thou bid me remember that day, by all thy days, O Despot?
What does it matter now that I hate thee no more?
I know not what new spell was heaved about me by the mighty mouth that breathes all the fear-
ful gales of life,
But this I do remember, that my soul became a cage full of nightingales and her hand opened
the door and they flew away in the azure of thy heavens in a long thrill of song.
And this also I do remember, that my heart in which every scythe had reaped till it was noth-
ing but a barren desolation, bloomed up suddenly in all thy apple blossoms, in all thy
almond trees, in all the flowers of thy orchards and of thy gardens, O Spring.
And I could not throw out of it its myriad flowers, for she had laid her hand on my heart and I
dared not break open the gentle gate of her fingers.
And so those flowers remained in me and left in me their fragrance and their pollen, and I grew
happy and wiser and older in the eternity of that moment.
I grew wiser that she might keep her illusions, and I grew older that I might see more of her
youth, but I was happy, for I held her quivering spirit in my trembling hands, like a frail
crystal bowl for the priceless, divine offering of my first tear.
And lo! something broke within me, in the untrodden and unexplored recesses of me (was it a
chain, was it a wall?) and I was free, and I was free from myself,
Free to give me to a new dungeon, free to sell me to a new bondage, I who until then had had
about me only the fetters of my pride.
But what do I care, O Spring, and what dost thou care now that I hate thee no more?

* * *

Again the flame I had tried to smother blazed forth from the innest hearths of my being and
my spirit grew lighter,
Every bird, every butterfly that flew away carried forth one of my unbound thoughts.
And I broke the spell of the abyss and my soul rose with the vapors of thy waters and the breath
of thy mountains and the fogs of thy valleys and the fragrance of thy flowers towards the
Dream that is hidden by the dazzling light of the sun.

There must have been in me, in the silence and darkness of me, a stranded god of old that had fallen asleep in the first spring of the world. And she awoke him with a kiss.

Why, why? Was it because it was spring and spring was different to her, or because we were both two pilgrims journeying together to the same shrine, I to burn the last offerings of my fading youth and she to depose the first garland of hers?

What does it matter, O Spring, now that I hate thee no more?

She kissed me and I awoke; again I awoke in the old land of beauty and song I had dwelled in since the day I knew the first word I spoke, and again my lips were unsealed by the uncrushable swelling of the rising paean to thee, O thou who art greater than life.

And again I became all-knowing and all-powerful,

The maker of wonders, the weaver of wreaths, the giver of treasures and kingdoms, the killer of dragons and the builder of temples and dreams,

And I spun with my nimble fingers the rays of the setting sun to make an aureole for her dark hair,

And I embroidered into the green foliage the chaste languor of the blue sky and there I set her head and contemplated in adoration the first masterpiece of my new handiwork.

And I said unto her: Lo, of all her flowers, Spring has given the rose to Love and the myrtle to the one that is greater, but unto thee that art between both and vowed and fated to both, I shall give the flower that grows unsown in the wilderness and was never plucked, was never laid on the altars and the tombs and the cradles, I shall give thee the thistle, sharp and pungent and bristling like a flame of raised swords.

* * *

And so it was that the lure of spring came again upon me, and I understood it and loved it and made amends and repentance for my hatred.

For she, this new Spring of mine and of the world that is to be mine was not false and decayed, She was not vanity and decoy,

She was not proffering to ignoble lovers the wiles of her lust,

But she was offering to all the children of life and all the warriors of the world the abundant milk of her overflowing motherly breasts and the balsam of her love.

* * *

But shall I sing of love now, I who could only sing to the tune of the clarions of war?

And shall I forget for a woman my black frothing horse that neighs after the twanging arrows in the wind?

And shall I not lose my strength when her arms shall encircle me where thou hast girt me with the sword. O Gea, my mother immortal?

"Sing Me to Sleep . . ."

When in my night like gaunt, gray phantoms rise
    The wild-eyed hours of brooding reverie,
If in my heart a sudden anguish cries
    That thou also hast passed away from me,

If I but think that one regretful sigh
    Thy joyless love has breathed unaware,
I know not what a barren will to die
    Dissolves my strength into a mute despair.

Oh, if upon thy breast I could then lay
    My weary head and hear thee sing again
That sad, sweet song, and as it dies away
    Exhale my spirit in its last refrain!

Utopia

Tis writ, and I believe with all my power,
    That a great day shall come, O Master, when,
Even as from a putrid clod a flower,
    So in thy heart shall bloom the love of men, —

A day when sweet and noble tasks shall hallow
    These charnels where thy slaves now drudge and plod,
And thou no more a groveling swine shalt wallow
    Amid the puddles of their sweat and blood, —

A day when shall thy soldiers cease their slaughters,
    No more thy name shall widows execrate,
When shall grow chaste thy meretricious daughters
    And thy abandoned sons regenerate,

When thy grandchildren shall not know what lust is,
    Nor shall thy festering sins corrode their youth,
When thy lawmakers shall believe in justice,
    Yea, and thy priests shall seek and preach the truth, —

A day when thy old parents from the gutter
    Shall beg no more thine alms as they do now,
And thou, withal, shalt earn thy bread and butter
    By thine own labor's sweat upon thy brow; —

A day shall come when gold shall not enthrall thee,
    When theft and murder cease to be thy rule;
So I, who call thee now a friend, shall call thee,
    Forsooth, a true and upright man,
                                "Thou fool!"

THE WELL OF THE GODS

I

I know a well engraved with mystic runes
    Within a clump of poplars in a dale,
Where sweetest are the shadows of the noons
    And from the hills winds down the shepherd's trail.

The fount that gurgles in its limpid pool,
    Not thousand years nor thousands have dispersed,
And is so clear its water, and so cool,
    That all who look in it become athirst.

I love its quaint, round mirror at twilight,
    And as in it for my own face I search,
Methinks I see instead an anchorite
    In some old fresco of a Roman church.

And as along its walls like lizards creep
    The quivering arabesques of green and gold,
I hear a flute-like voice from out the deep,
    As of a strayed and lonely faun of old,
Who, when the gods migrated, lay in his hold asleep.

II

Only the rain doth in its depths descend,
    A jagged shred of sky and few tree tops;
But if Scirocco peradventure rend
    The palisaded rampart of the copse,

All of the mountain's breath, the gorge's boom,
    The crash of riven trees the tempest tore,
Would then be cast into the startled gloom
    And fill it all with echoes and uproar.

But when into its lap of velvet throws
    A group of stars the eventide of June,
And brighter in its magic mirror glows
    The silver sickle of the crescent moon,

When to the sleepy lark that faintly sings
    The clear, full-throated nightingale responds,
The blent accord of light and music rings
    Like bounding pearls into a bowl of bronze.
Love, in the well then flutter my garlands and thy wings.

III

Chalice and urn of all the gods of yore,
    Is in thy bosom such a wizardry.
That he inherits all thy ancient lore
    Who drinks the nectar they forgot in thee.

Thus I, who come a pilgrim from the hill,
    Ere I ascend unto a loftier goal,
Do drink of thee with avid lips, to fill
    Out of thy plenitude of songs my soul.

And lo! meseems that in the golden sheen
    Centaurs and Satyrs gambol in the grove,
And Nymphs and Naiads on thy border lean
    To sing the strains of a forgotten love.

And though into the heavens of pure sapphire
    Only the shepherd's lay soars high and clear,
With wistful ears of rapture and desire
    Breathless with wonder I can almost hear
Attuning their eclogue the laureled Virgil's lyre.

The Last Nickel

I

Cold and silent and myriad-eyed with the chills of dead things, with the silence of the things that are eternal and with the tremulous palpitation of the stars was the night, the holy night of my awakening and my despair.

I stood before the blazing windows of Tiffany. Frozen tears of shame and pain and wrath, frozen clots of murder blood, frozen drops of poison were the pearls, the rubies, the emeralds that glittered and winked, malevolent as the first hoar-frost upon a bed of flowers, as the grin of a mortal enemy, as the leer of lustful eyes that glare into eyes that are full of tears.

I had just kissed Her for the first time, perhaps the eternal troth, perhaps the everlasting farewell, so I looked not into the mirage of the hell-lit window, for I was thinking.

I was thinking of her eyes, wide open, frightened and full of promises, retreating slowly like the phosphorescent haze of dreams into the blackness of the tenement hall-way;

I was thinking of the gasping windows gulping the thin breath of the dying trees through the stuffed fire escapes;

I was thinking of the room where She now stood, wonder-eyed, loosening her hair, and of the poor virginal bed by the strangled airshaft where She would lie awake all night thinking of me.

I was thinking of all She would hear through the endless night;

The incessant wailing of the sick child above, and the maddening rhythm of the cradle rocked by a nerveless, unstrung hand,

The heavy snoring of the man below, frightful like a death rattle,

The stealthy, cautious steps of the belated girl and the grumbling curses and the muffled weeping,

The foul-worded, blow-crashing quarrel of the drunken couple that would tear through the partition wall,

And the faint echo of my faltering good-by, and the startling sound of her own sighs.

And I was thinking also of the red ribbon She had worn for so many weeks, ever since I knew Her, and of the broken-lipped step of her doorway, and of my last nickel, which was dearer to me than all the gems in that demoniacal window and which I was about to throw away, an immense and unknown sacrifice, for the love of Her.

II

But even as I was about to cast it solemnly and religiously away, with the rite of the priest who
 drops the offering into the fire and the vast gesture of the sower who scatters the seeds of
 the bread, two men approached me, two shadows of the light of the gems.

Said one: "For two whole days I have not eaten. No one believes me, and if you also do not, I
 shall die. Give me a nickel in the name of Jesus and of the One you love and I will pray
 God for your happiness and your salvation."

I looked at him and in his eyes, where the pupils had been. I saw the yellow prints of the bony
 finger tips of hunger.

Said the other: "I know that I am drunk, but I need more. Give me the nickel and I will drink it
 to your health and joy."

I looked at him also and in his eyes, where the sunlight had been, I saw the smothering embers
 of his soul.

But neither in the eyes of the one, nor in the eyes of the other, saw I reflected the fierce glow of
 the jewels in the nearby window. They both wanted my nickel, my only nickel, my last
 nickel, my cheap, finger-worn nickel — a loaf of bread — a glass of whisky — no more!

III

Chuckled aloud in my ears the fiend that lurked in the scintillating window, the fiend that kin-
 dles all the evil fires of the world, and said: "Behold, thou who hast only a nickel art now
 become a dispenser of life and death and an arbiter of destinies. But thou canst satisfy but
 one man, and thou hast not the wisdom of a Solomon. Whichever man thou givest it to,
 not knowing whether the one be truly hungry or the other really need it more, thy gift
 shall accrue to the injustice of the world. Throw it away, then, for her sake, as thou desirest,
 build with it a little mound of thine own happiness, and not a mountam of thy conceit."

I thought of the sweatshop where She was going to work again the next day . . .

Then the angel in me spoke: "Nay, give it to the hungry one. If She were here by thee, thou
 knowest that thou wouldst give it to him. What greater deed canst thou do for the love of
 Her to-night? Give it to him, he will live because he shall eat and the other will not die,
 because he will not drink the last goblet of poison. Thou shalt thus save two men."

Then said the devil in me: "Remember what was said of old: 'We asked for bread and ye gave us
 a stone.' They understood not the symbol then, nor would they understand it now. They
 know not what to do with a stone, a good heavy stone, a fine hard stone that would go as
 far as their hunger, their thirst and their manhood. Preach, then, no more idle sermons and
 give it to the drunken one. He will die of delirium and the other of hunger. Thou shalt thus
 kill two brutes."

I saw the malevolent glitter, the leer and the sneer of the diamonds, the pearls, the rubies, the
 emeralds in the hell-lit window, and I saw in the eyes of the two men nothing but the
 greed and the fever for my nickel, my last nickel, for my cheap, finger-worn nickel . . .

And I gave it to one of them.

The Republic

The king had said: "By right divine
As old as God's own laws are old,
All that you have, all that you hold,
All that you think and do is mine.

"I own forever and control
Your house, your field, your ox, your wife,
So, I shall rule your mortal life
And my good liege, the pope, your soul.

"Obey, then, both; do not rebel,
For, should you rise against our will,
You'll have, in this world, my Bastille,
And in the other world his hell."

So said the king. And then there came,
Aglow with anger and with steel,
A goddess of the common weal,
With eyes of fire and hair of flame.

Not hers the wisdom which decrees
That time alone must wrong allay,
Not hers the craven heart to pray
And barter liberty for peace;

Not hers the fear to hesitate
When shame and misery cry out —
Love has no patience, truth no doubt,
And right and justice cannot wait.

So, loud into the midnight air
She rang the tocsin's weird alarm,
She called, and as by potent charm
From its mysterious haunt and lair,

The Mob, the mightiest judge of all,
To hear the rights of Man came out,
And every word became a shout,
And every shout a cannon ball.

Against the castle walls the picks
She raised and planted there her flags,
Against the ermine hurled the rags,
The torch against the crucifix,

The guillotine against the rope,
And ere the eastern sky grew red,
Behold she flung the king's proud head
Upon the altars of the pope.

And when upon the great sunrise
Flew her disheveled victories
To all the lands, on all the seas,
Like angry eagles in the skies,

To ring the call of brotherhood
And hail mankind from shore to shore,
Wrapt in her splendid tricolor
The People's virgin bride she stood.

* * *

This was the dawn. But when the day
Wore out with all its festive songs,
And all the hearts, and all the tongues
Were stilled in wonder and dismay, —

When night with velvet-sandaled feet
Stole in her chamber's solitude,
Behold! she lay there naked, lewd,
A drunken harlot of the street,

With withered breasts and shaggy hair
Soiled by each wanton, frothy kiss,
Between a sergeant of police
And a decrepit millionaire.

The Funeral

I saw a funeral go by this morning, a black hearse driven by one black horse climbing slowly the
    silent street, the street unsouled and grief-stricken by the gray omens of the coming first
    snow.

No carriages followed the black hearse, no mourners walked behind it, no flowers were on the
    coffin, and my heart, my mad heart that divines everything, told me that no one was
    weeping in the great city.

I followed it with my unseeing eyes and then I turned to my love who stood by me at the win-
    dow (always with me, always by me shall be my love) and I wanted to kiss her to dispel
    the anguish of the gray morning and of the silent street and of the black hearse.

But my love held me away with her hand and said: "Nay, kiss me not now and speak not of our
    love, but let us go and follow that hearse, and throw some earth into the grave, for that is
    our forgotten brother that died yesterday."

And I said to my love: "Aye, my love, let us go and mourn for him, our unknown brother, so
    that some day someone shall also walk behind our biers. At least one, at least one . . ."

But my love answered again: "Nay, what will it matter to us then? We shall be two in the cof-
    fin. Let us go and mourn for him, just for him, only for the sake of him, only for the sake
    of sorrow and death and tears.

"For we have cursed and fought and hated enough, my love, and it will do us good to weep."

And we followed the lonely hearse up the silent street, the street unsouled and grief-stricken by
    the gray omens of the coming first snow,

And we looked not at each other, and we did not speak.

To Joseph J. Ettor

On His 27th Birthday

Well, Joe, my good friend, though we cannot pretend
    That we're happy we still can regale,
We can laugh and be merry, though claret and sherry

Are so scarce to us, even in jail;
But although our good wine is the prison's foul brine
    And the hangman's our welcoming host,
Let us think it Chianti and quaff it a-plenty
    While for you I revise my old toast.

Let us drink a new toast to the dear Woolen trust,
    To the legions of "Country and God,"
To the great Christian cause and the wise, noble laws,
    And to all who cry out for our blood;
Let us drink to the health of the old Commonwealth,
    To the Bible and code in one breath,
And let's so propitiate both the church and the state
    That they'll grant us a cheerful, quick death.

For altho' you are brave, you'll admit that the grave
    Has much better surroundings than these,
As we'll hear there no more the hard slam of the door
    And the clank of the terrible keys;
Even as I, though I'm game, must admit just the same,
    When I think of my love and my home,
That my heart is oppressed and my soul is distressed
    By the thought of the years yet to come.

And I cannot conceive all the years we must grieve
    For the dream that no hope can revive,
And my heart seems to sink when I tremblingly think
    Of the One who will mourn me alive;
For when last I did gaze on her sweet, saint-like face,
    That forever from me would be barred,
Well, the only good way I could keep looking gay
    Was to think of a nice big graveyard.

Yes, I know it is good, in some soul-stirring mood
    To drive out all these sullen complaints,
And I know it feels great to believe that our fate
    Will be that of the martyrs and saints.
But what joy is in truth if our passionate youth
    Like an underground runnel must flow
That no thirst ever slakes, but just feeds the gray lakes
    Of the kingdoms of silence and woe?

Nay, 'tis all silly fuss, there's no wisdom in us
    To renounce to the brunt of the strife;
We were wrought on the fire and to love and desire
    And to fight and to sing is our life.
So, should we many a year be immured alive here,
    Now that you're twenty-seven, old mate,
The best wish I can make for your own and my sake
    Is that never you be twenty-eight.

And so, here's to the hope for the trap and the rope
    As the best for us sure is the worst,
And because I am older and you are the bolder,
    Here's a health that they hang me the first;
For, should justice be shunned, both on earth and beyond,
    After bidding to you my farewell,
I would fain as your scout be the first to find out
    And the first to receive you in hell.

THE SERMON ON THE COMMON

Then it came to pass that the people, having heard that he had come, assembled on the Common to listen unto his words.

And they came from all the parts of the earth, the Syrians and the Armenians, the Thracians and the Tartars, the Jews, the Greeks and the Romans, the Iberians and the Gauls and the Angles and Huns and the Hibernians and Scythians, even from the deserts of sands to the deserts of ice, they came to listen unto his words.

And he, seeing the multitudes, opened his mouth, and taught them, saying,

Blessed are the strong in freedom's spirit: for theirs is the kingdom of the earth.

Blessed are they that mourn their martyred dead: for they shall avenge them upon their murderers and be comforted.

Blessed are the rebels: for they shall reconquer the earth.

Blessed are they which do hunger and thirst after equality: for they shall eat the fruit of their labor.

Blessed are the strong: for they shall not taste the bitterness of pity.

Blessed are the sincere in heart: for they shall see truth.

Blessed are they that do battle against wrong: for they shall be called the children of Liberty.

Blessed are they which are persecuted for equality's sake: for theirs is the glory of the brotherhood of man.

Blessed are ye when the scribes of the press shall revile you, and the doctors of the law, politicians, policemen, judges and priests shall call you criminals, thieves and murderers and shall say all manner of evil against you falsely, for the sake of Justice.

Rejoice, then, and be exceedingly glad; for so they persecuted, reviled, cursed, chained, jailed, poisoned, hanged, crucified, burned, beheaded and shot all the seers, the apostles and the warriors of humanity that were before you, for the sake of freedom.

Ye are the power of the earth, the foundations of society, the thinkers and the doers of all things good and all things fair and useful, the makers and dispensers of all the bounties and the joys and the happiness of the world, and if ye fold your mighty arms, all the life of the world stands still and death hovers on the darkened abodes of man.

Ye are the light of the world. There was darkness in all the ages when the torch of your will did not blaze forth, and the past and the future are full of the radiance that cometh from your eyes.

Ye are eternal, even as your father, labor, is eternal, and no power of time and dissolution can prevail against you.

Ages have come and gone, kingdoms and powers and dynasties have risen and fallen, old glories and ancient wisdoms have been turned into dust, heroes and sages have been forgotten and many a mighty and fearsome god has been hurled into the lightless chasms of oblivion.

But ye, Plebs, Populace, People, Rabble, Mob, Proletariat, live and abide forever.

* * *

Think not that I am come to destroy the law: I am not come to destroy, but to fulfill through you what the prophets of mankind have presaged from the beginning.

For verily I say unto you, While man lives and labors, nothing can destroy the eternal law of progress which after each advancing step bids him further.

Therefore, say not unto yourselves, even as the priests and scribes and doctors of the law and fools and hypocrites say, This is the goal which was destined unto us and no further shall we go.

For even if there be before you the uplifted arms of terror and the smoking altars of murder enshrined in a gaunt temple of gibbets and fierce with shrieks of curses, ye must pass beyond.

For your feet are like the unrolling of the endless scrolls of time, — not even night and silence and death can stop their march forward and upward, ever to a farther and loftier goal.

And, lo, ye shall never arrive because never shall ye cease going.

Whosoever, therefore, shall break one jot or one tittle of this law shall be called the least in the kingdom of man, but whosoever shall do and teach it, the same shall be called great in the kingdom of man.

Ye have heard that it was said by them of all times who toil not but do live of your toil, Thou shalt not rebel against thy master.

But I say unto you that whosoever soweth the seeds of patience the same shall reap the harvest of shame.

They said unto you, Question not the right of your masters to reign over you and command you. They shall have your sweat and your tears, aye, and even your blood and your life, and ye shall serve them in reverence and awe, for their power upon you is of God.

And again they said unto, you, Give your masters the labor of your hands and the worship of your hearts, give them the fruits of your orchards, the grains of your fields, the flowers of your gardens and all things made by the labor of your hands and by the thought of your brain, and withhold not aught from your masters, lest your masters' law and the curse of your masters' God be upon you.

And again they said unto you, Bend your kness and worship your chains, kiss the whip that lashes you, bless the heel that crushes you, revere the yoke that weighs upon your neck, bury your forehead in the dirt whence ye came and whither ye shall return.

Do not cry, do not complain, do not grumble, do not think, do not hope,

Be humble, resigned, patient, submissive, lowly and prone even as a beast of burden, lest ye have the gaol in this life and gehenna in the life to come.

And again they said unto you, Resist not evil, for all spirit of disobedience and unsubmission issueth from the enemy of peace. Therefore if your masters, or your masters' servants smite you on the right check, turn unto them the other also, and if they take away from you the heritage of your fathers, give unto them also the birthright of your children.

All this and more than this they said unto you before I came, but now that I am come, a new evangel shall be proclaimed unto you, that your souls may be renovated and purified in the fire of the new salvation which is not peace but war.

Therefore I say unto you, Banish fear from your hearts, dispel the mists of ignorance from your minds, arm your yearning with your strength, your vision with your will, and open your eyes and behold.

Do not moan, do not submit, do not kneel, do not pray, do not wait.

Think, dare, do, rebel, fight — ARISE!

It is not true that ye are condemned to serve and suffer in shame forever;

It is not true that injustice, iniquity, hunger, misery, abjection, depravity, hatred, theft, murder and fratricide are eternal;

There is no destiny that the will of man cannot break;

There are no chains of iron that other iron cannot destroy;

There is nothing that the power of your arms, lighted by the power of your mind, cannot transform and reconstruct and remake.

Arise, then, ye men of the plough and the hammer, the helm and the lever, and send forth to the four winds of the earth your new proclamation of freedom which shall be the last and shall abide forevermore.

Through you, through your united, almighty strength, order shall become equity, law shall become liberty, duty shall become love and religion shall become truth.

Through you the man-beast shall die and the man be born;

Through you the dark, bloody chronicles of the brute shall cease and the story of man shall begin.

Through you, by the power of your brain and hand,

All the predictions of the prophets,

All the wisdom of the sages,

All the dreams of the poets,

All the hopes of the heroes,

All the visions of the martyrs,

All the prayers of the saints,

All the crushed, tortured, strangled, maimed and murdered ideals of the ages, and all the glorious destinies of mankind shall become a triumphant and everlasting reality in the name of labor and bread and love, the great threefold truth forever.

And lo and behold, my brothers, this shall be called the revolution.

* * *

Thus spake the man to the assembled multitude that had come from all the lands, over all the waters of the earth, and they listened unto him and received his words, and the dawn began to rise in their hearts, and they praised the announcer with the cheers of their mouths and they blessed him with the tears of their eyes.

But when the multitude dispersed to return to their labors and to their strifes, the dark figures that make darker the shadows of the night held council against the truth-bearer for the words that he had spoken.

And the scribe said, Verily, he is a law-breaker.

And the money changer said, Aye, and he is a fool.

And the judge said, He is a wrong-doer.

And the sage said, He is possessed of a devil.

And the chronicler said, He is a primitive sinner.

And the wise man said, He is a profligate.

And the priest said, He is a blasphemer.

And they all croaked in chorus, He is an enemy of society, of civilization, of religion and mankind. Law and order must be upheld and our sacred institutions must be preserved. We must do away with him.

And they did away with him. But nobody knows to this day whether they sent him to prison or to Parliament.

THE PEACEFUL HOUR

This is the hour of peace, the hour of all the things I love.

The things I love are the things that are my own forever, the things that shall never be taken away from me.

They are not the things that I have made, for nothing have I made to myself,

They are not the things I fashioned with my many-tooled hands,

Not the things I have brought forth out of the smoke of my pipe, in the gathering dusk of my half-closed eyelids,

Not the things I saw far away and brought nearer, for no burden-bearer and no messenger am I to myself,

Not the things I revived, for nothing of mine ever died,

But the things that were given to me, the things I wanted not and did not ask and did not covet, but were simply given to me unearned and undeserved because I needed them and knew it not.

For they alone are forever my own, not because I must fight to keep them, but because the givers will never take them back from me.

I love the black bread the wayfarer shared with me at the fountain and which I ate not for hunger but for the joy of him,

I love the wine the stranger offered me at the tavern by the roadside,

And the tune of the old hand-organ under my window,

And the kiss of the two child-lips while I was sleeping,

And the song of my sweetheart who is sewing in the warm sunlight,

And the loud cries of my baby that wants to be fed,

Yea, and that man who is passing by on the sidewalk yonder, whoever, whatever he be and wherever he goes in this hour of peace.

SAMNITE CRADLE SONG

Lullaby, baby, mamma's own child!
Who sang the evil dirge about thee?
Thou camest in March time, wee as the tart
Berries of hedge thorns, pale, as the wild
Roses that have a wasp in their heart.
Who has to thee the witchy words spoken?
Who read to thee the malevolent star?
Who cast on thee the spell of the dead?
A hunchbacked wizard thy cradle has broken,
A lame old fairy embittered my teat,

And the blind priest with unblessed water wet
At the font thy poor, innocent head.
Thou art so sleepy, but numb are my arms;
Thou art so cold, but chilled is my breath;
Thou art so hungry, but dry is my breast.
Lullaby, hush-a-by, baby mine, rest,
Sleep for thy mother, who is tired unto death.

Lullaby, baby! The corn was so full,
The vines were so heavy, the season so pleasant,
And happy, so happy, the heart of the peasant,
Who was preparing and sweeping the bin
For the new wheat that was bristling so fine,
While his nude youngster was laughing within
The casks he was scrubbing to fill with new wine.
But God dislikes them whose heart is content,
God loves only them who starve and bewail;
And so he sent us the wind and the hail.
All has been carried away by landslides;
All has been buried beneath the brown mire;
All has been ruined by storms and by tides,
Nor vineyards nor orchards the water did leave.
The mice now dance in the empty meal keeve;
The ashes are cold of the last cauldron fire;
The dams and the flood-traps the torrent has torn;
And poor we! the mill that once ground our corn
Now grinds away the last hope of the land.
Lullaby, baby, the morning is nigh.
Hush-a-by, baby, thou must understand,
The tale of my woe is as long as thy cry.

Lullaby, baby, thy grandfather plowed
And thy father mowed the grain,
And thy mother winnowed the chaff,
And at evening many a spool
Spinned with spindle and distaff,
Threads of hemp and threads of wool.
But granddaddy was broken and bowed,
The land was hard, the winters were cold;
But thy father was twenty years old,
So they took him away and sent him to war.
One was old and one was young,

One was weak and one was strong,
One was too tired to till the sod,
One was fresh in the heart of spring.
So thy grandpa was killed by God,
And thy daddy by the king.

Lullaby, hush-a-by, baby mine, sleep,
    Lullaby, softer than thine is their bed!
Mother will sing thee, mother'll not weep,
    Mother'll not mourn for the dead.

Lullaby, baby, grow strong and brave!
They are no longer hungry now;
Only us two the bad luck smote.
The gravedigger took away the goat,
For digging an eight-foot grave;
The curate has taken the sow,
For saying mass by the biers;
And the Government for its toll
Has taken the earrings from mine ears,
Lullaby, baby, they took our all,
The walnut chest, the iron bed,
The silver brooch, the marriage ring,
The black fichu in which I was wed;
I have not even a scarf to mourn
And honor my young love forlorn
And the faith I swore to him.
I have only the sack of straw,
The bident with the broken horn,
And the medal which the law
Has sent to thee, an iron thing,
Which in his honor bears the trace
Of his young blood upon one face,
And on the other side the grace
Of God about our gracious king.

Lullaby, hush-a-by, baby mine, sleep,
    Lullaby, softer than thine is their bed!
Mother will sing thee, mother'll not weep,
    Mother'll not mourn for the dead.

Lullaby, baby, the winter is near,
The mountains put on their clean hood of snow.
What shall I do? Where shall I go?
In the sieve there is no more flour;
In the bin there is no more coal;
In the jug there is no more oil.
What shall I do, my desperate soul?
Am I to die of hunger and cold,
Or beg for bread from door to door,
Or be a wanton about the inns?
Ah, what do I care what I shall be,
What do I care, so you do not die?
My grief shall stop where your joy begins
And our good day shall surely come by.
And when it comes, and I am in my grave
Or past the age of thy pride or blame,
If I keep true to all that aid me,
Give back a hundred for one they gave,
But if I rear thee with sweets and with shame,
Lullaby, hush-a-by, harken, my life,
For every dollar of silver they paid me,
Give back a stab with your father's keen knife.

Lullaby, hush-a-by, baby mine, sleep,
        Lullaby, softer than thine is their bed!
Mother will sing thee, mother'll not weep,
        Mother'll not mourn for the dead.

Lullaby, baby, the rope is so frayed
That down the well soon the bucket will dart;
The whip is broken, the yoke torn in twain;
But see, how sharp is the hatchet's blade!
The ass has broken away from the cart,
The hound has shaken and slipped from the chain
And I am singing away my fierce heart
Just for the rage of the song, not the pain.
Behold, the dawn fingers the shadows dispel,
Soon will the sun peep at thee from the hill;
The cocks are crowing, the starlings grow shrill.
Wait, and my song with the matin's glad bell
Shall fill the morning with omens of glee.
For now no longer I sing unto thee,

Mamma's own wolflet, the tale of my woe,
But now that the sun is near, my man-boy,
The night is gone, and my sorrow will go;
List to my prophecy, vengeance and joy.

Lullaby, baby, look! Our great king
With all his princes and barons and sons,
Goes to the church to pray to the Lord.
Ring all the bells! Fire all the guns!
For all the chapter is wearing the cope,
And the bishop himself will sing the high mass.
How came this vision to me, my wild hope?
How came this wonderful fortune to pass?
Behold, the bishop lifts up the grail;
The king is kneeling upon the gray stone;
The trumpets hush, the organ heaves deep:
"*Te Deum laudamus* . . . We praise thee, O Lord . . .
For all thy mercies, Lord, hail! all hail!"
Hush-a-by, lullaby, listen! Don't sleep!
Lullaby, hush-a-by, mark well my word!
Thou shalt grow big. Don't tremble! Don't fail!
The holy wafer is but kneaded dough;
The king is but flesh like the man with the hoe;
The axe is of iron, the same as the sword;
This I do tell thee and this I do sing.
And if thou livest with sweat and with woe,
Grow like a man, not a saint, nor a knave;
Do not be good, but be strong and be brave,
With the fangs of a wolf and the faith of a dog.
Die not the death of a soldier or slave,
Like thy grandfather who died in a bog,
Like thy poor father who rots in the rain.
But for this womb that has borne thee in pain,
For these dry breasts thou hast tortured so long,
For the despair of my life, my lost hope,
And for this song of the dawn that I sing
Die like a man by the axe or the rope,
Spit on their God and stab our good king.

Sleep no more, sleep no more! Show me you know,
Show me you listen, answer my sob!
Drink my blood, drain my heart! Just one sign . . . so!
Bite my breast, bite it harder, mother's tiger cub!

The Cage

In the middle of the great greenish room stood the green iron cage.

All was old, and cold and mournful, ancient with the double antiquity of heart and brain in the great greenish room.

Old and hoary was the man who sat upon the faldstool, upon the fireless and godless altar,

Old were the tomes that mouldered behind him on the dusty shelves,

Old was the painting of an old man that hung above him;

Old the man upon his left who awoke with his cracked voice the dead echoes of dead centuries, old the man upon his right who wielded a wand; and old all those who spoke to him and listened to him before and around the green iron cage.

Old were the words they spoke, and their faces were drawn and white and lifeless, without expression or solemnity; like the ikons of old cathedrals.

For of naught they knew, but of what was written in the old, yellow books. And all the joys and the pains and the loves and hatreds and furies and labors and strifes of man, all the fierce and divine passions that battle and rage in the heart of man, never entered into the great greenish room but to sit in the green iron cage.

Senility, dullness and dissolution were all around the green iron cage, and nothing was new and young and alive in the great room, except the three men who were in the cage.

* * *

Throbbed and thundered and clamored and roared outside of the great greenish room the terrible whirl of life, and most pleasant was the hymn of its mighty polyphony to the listening ears of the gods.

Whirred the wheels of the puissant machines, rattled and clanked the chains of the giant cranes, crashed the falling rocks, the riveters crepitated and glad and sonorous was the rhythm of the bouncing hammers upon the loud-throated anvils.

Like the chests of wrathfully toiling Titans, heaved and sniffed and panted the sweaty boilers, like the hissing of dragons sibilated the jets of steam, and the sirens of the workshops shrieked like angry hawks flapping above the crags of a dark and fathomless chasm.

The files screeched and the trains thundered, the wires hummed, the dynamos buzzed, the fires crackled; and like a thunderclap from the cyclopean forge roared the blasts of the mines.

Wonderful and fierce was the mighty symphony of the world, as the terrible voices of metal and fire and water cried out into the listening ears of the gods the furious song of human toil.

Out of the chaos of sound, welded in the unison of one will to sing, rose clear and nimble the divine accord of the hymn.

> Out of the canyons of the mountains,
> Out of the whirlpools of the dams,
> Out of the entrails of the earth,
> Out of the yawning gorges of hell,

From the land and the sea and the sky

And from whatever comes bread and wealth and joy,

And from the peaceful abodes of men rose majestic and fierce, louder than the roar of the volcano and the bellow of the typhoon, the anthem of human labor to the fatherly justice of the Sun.

But in the great greenish room there was nothing but the silence of dead centuries and of ears that listen no more; and none heard the mighty call of life that roared outside, save the three men who were in the cage.

* * *

All the good smells, the wholesome smells, the healthy smells of life and labor were outside the great room.

The smell of rain upon the grass and of the flowers consumed by their love for the stars;

The heavy smell of smoke that coiled out of myriads of chimneys of ships and factories and homes,

The dry smell of sawdust and the salty smell of the iron filings;

The odor of magazines and granaries and warehouses, the kingly smell of argosies and the rich scent of market places, so dear to the women of the race;

The smell of new cloth and new linen, the smell of soap and water, and the smell of newly printed paper,

The smell of grains and hay and the smell of stables, the warm smell of cattle and sheep that Virgil loved;

The smell of milk and wine and plants and metals,

And all the good odors of the earth and of the sea and of the sky, and the fragrance of fresh bread, sweetest aroma of the world, and the smell of human sweat, most holy incense to the divine nostrils of the gods, and all the Olympian perfumes of the heart and the brain and the passions of men were outside of the great greenish room.

But within the old room there was nothing but the smell of old books and the dust of things decayed, and the suffocated exhalations of old graves, and the ashen odor of dissolution and death.

Yet all the sweetness of all the wholesome odors of the world outside was redolent in the breath of the three men in the cage.

Like crippled eagles fallen were the three men in the cage, and like little children who look into a well to behold the sky were the men that looked down upon them.

No more would they rise to their lofty eyries, no more would they soar above the snowcapped mountains — yet, tho' their pinions were broken, nothing could dim the fierce glow of their eyes that knew all the altitudes of heaven.

Strange it was to behold the men in the cage while life clamored outside, and strange it seemed to them that they should be there because of what dead men had written in old books.

So of naught did they think but of the old books and the green cage.

Thought they: "All things are born, grow, decay, die and are forgotten. Surely all that is in this room will pass away. But what will endure the longer, the folly that was written into the old books or the madness that was beaten into the bands of this cage?

"Which of these two powers has enthralled us, the thought of the dead men who wrote the old books, or the labor of living men who have wrought this cage?"

Long and intently they thought, but they found no answer.

* * *

But one of the men in the cage, whose soul was tormented by the fiercest fire of hell, which is the yearning after the Supreme Truth, spoke and said unto his comrades:

"Aye, brothers, all things die and pass away, yet nothing is truly and forever dead until each one of the living has thrown a regretless handful of soil into its grave.

"Many a book has been written since these old books were written, and many a proverb of the sage has became the jest of the fool, yet this cage still stands as it stood for numberless ages.

"What is it, then, that made it of metal more enduring than the printed word?

"Which is its power to hold us here?

"Brothers, it is the things we love that enslave us,

"Brothers, it is the things we yearn for that subdue us,

"Brothers, it is not hatred for the things that are, but love for the things that are to be that make us slaves.

"And what man is more apt to become a thrall, brothers, and to be locked in a green iron cage, than he who yearns the most for the Supreme of the things that are to be — he who most craves for Freedom?

"And what subtle and malignant power, save this love of loves, could be in the metal of this cage that it is so mad to emprison us?"

So spoke one of the men to the other two, and then, out of the silence of the aeons spoke into his tormented soul the metallic soul of the cage.

* * *

"Iron, the twin brother of fire, the first born out of the matrix of the earth, the witness everlasting to the glory of thy labor am I, O Man!

"Nor for this was I meant, O Man! Not to imprison thee, but to set thee free and sustain thee in thy strife and in thy toil.

"I was to lift the pillars of the Temple higher than the mountains;

"I was to break down and bore through all the barriers of the world to open the way to thy triumphant chariot.

"All the treasures and all the bounties of the earth was I to give as on offering into thy hands, and all its forces and powers to bring chained like crouching dogs at thy feet.

"Hadst thou not sinned against the nobility of my nature and my destiny, hadst thou not humiliated me, an almighty warrior, to become the lackey of gold, I would have never risen against thee and enslaved thee, O Man!

"While I was hoe and ploughshare and sword and axe and scythe and hammer, I was the first artificer of thy happiness; but the day I was beaten into the first lock and the first key, I became fetters and chains to thy hands and thy feet, O Man!

"My curse is thy curse, O Man, and even if thou shouldst pass out of the wicket of this cage, never shalt thou be free until thou returnest me to the joy of labor.

"O Man, bring me back into the old smithy, purify me again with the holy fire of the forge, lay me again on the mother breast of the anvil, beat me again with the old honest hammer — O Man, remould me with thy wonderful hands into an instrument of thy toil,

> Remake of me the sword of thy justice,
> Remake of me the tripod of thy worship,
> Remake of me the sickle for thy grain,
> Remake of me the oven for thy bread,
> And the andirons for thy peaceful hearth, O Man!
> And the trestles for the bed of thy love, O Man!
> And the frame of thy joyous lyre, O Man!"

* * *

Thus spake to one of the three men, out of the silence of centuries, the metallic soul of the cage.

And he listened unto its voice, and while it was still ringing in his soul — which was tormented by the fiercest fire of hell, which is the yearning after the supreme truth (Is it Death? Is it Love?) — there arose one man in the silent assembly of old men that were around the iron cage.

And that man was the most hoary of all, and most bent and worn and crushed was he under the heavy weight of the great burden he bore without pride and without joy.

He arose and addressing himself — I know not whether to the old man that sat on the black throne, or to the old books that were mouldering behind him, or to the picture that hung above him — he said (and dreary as a wind that moans through the crosses of an old graveyard was his voice):

"I will prove to you that these three men in the cage are criminals and murderers and that they ought to be put to death."

* * *

Love, it was then that I heard for the first time the creak of the moth that was eating the old painting and the old books, and the worm that was gnawing the old bench, and it was then that I saw that all the old men around the great greenish room were dead.

They were dead like the old man in the painting, save that they still read the old books he could read no more, and still spoke and heard the old words he could speak and hear no more, and still passed the judgment of the dead, which he no more could pass, upon the mighty life of the world outside throbbed and thundered and clamored and roared the wonderful anthem of human labor to the fatherly justice of the Sun.

The Last Oracle

To Anne Sullivan Macy, teacher of Helen Keller.

I

Teacher, I who have sought in my fierce youth
In many an ancient scroll of obscure lore
The key-word to the dark, Medusean door
Behind which, on the grave of fear, stands truth;

And in my restless quest and desolate
The chariots of my warrior heart I drove,
Hurling in vain the rams of faith and love
Against the terrors of the mighty gate,

I knew not that the wisdom of this age
Had even now the fearful shrine unlocked,
Until, wayfarer of the world, I knocked
At thy remote and peaceful hermitage.

'Twas not the house of Silence, though no sound
Heard I within the lofty colonnade,
And yet meseemed that somewhere in the shade,
Something did stir, indefinite, profound;

Something that shook and tore the deepest strings
Of my stout heart — a Voice that only says
And does not speak, above the world's byways,
Dolorous like the beat of broken wings.

'Twas not the house of Darkness, yet though faint,
No worldly light I saw, but what did seem
The haze that lights at night the placid dream
Of children and the vision of the saint.

Therein stood I as he whose trembling lips
The last deep message of his prayer has said,
And fearfully awaits with drooping head
The blare of the supreme apocalypse.

Yet asked I not to see for the wan wraith
Of my wild youth that all the roads had tried,
Not for the sorrows of the Crucified,
Nor for the works of my all-suffering faith;

But for the One who waits earth-bound in chains
The greater flame of his first conquered spark,
To gain back, if he leap from out the dark,
The crown that heaven has stolen from his domains;

For Him I asked whose rebel soul was hurled
Into the deepest pit of burning fire,
Yet never ceased to battle and conspire
To render back to cheated Man his world;

And for the One upon whose back the yoke
And the feast tables of old Croesus stand,
And by the power of whose almighty hand,
Teacher, the seals that sealed the gate you broke.

II

I felt not sad, nor yet did I rejoice.
My life retreated to its last recess,
And then, from out the unfathomed nothingness
I heard the answer of the loneliest Voice.

The Voice that thou hast moulded with thy deft
And learned hands of love and firmly struck
Not in ignoble clay, but in the rock
That tides and bolts has braved, unmoved, uncleft.

The Voice thou didst reclaim from out the still
Empire whose gate no one before thee shook,
The Voice that has belied the crafty book,
Man's destinies to sing and to fulfill.

Said She: "My world is wider than the strength
Of thy sharp eyes can girdle and surround,
For in my night in which I see no bound,
I cannot walk the fullness of its length.

"But thou who canst behold and dost respond
Often unto the lures that guile thy soul,
No farther than thy gaze shall make thy goal
And pitch thy tent where started I beyond.

"For I no greater obstacles can meet
Than this, the voiceless dark which I explore,
And yet, how loud, like the sea's surging roar,
I hear the sunward march of countless feet.

"They go with me and I with them. But where,
They know not nor I cannot signify,
Oh, if I could but find the voice to cry
For me, the eyes to see, the ears to hear.

"If I could find the one to sally forth,
My vision and his strength their foes would rout,
And clear the way for them and lead them out
 Of bondage to the gardens of the earth.

"Whom shall I send? My heart has grown unsteady
In its long quest." — I bowed my head in pain . . .
Then in its battle armor leaped again
My warrior heart and answered: "Send me, Lady!"

III

Send me! Whatever in thy watchful night
Thou blessest, I shall blazon in the morn
And what thou cursest with thy withering scorn
Into the conquered ditches I shall smite.

Send me, send me! Thy words shall sear and cleave
Like trails of mighty armies through the land,
For thou alone canst see and understand
The destiny we only can achieve.

For though we had the truth, the tool, the word
To pit against our foemen's lies and gold,
No sacred name had we to stand and hold
Against the One whose cross has shaped their sword;

The One who sanctified their holocaust,
Whose words of peace our holy war have cursed,
Whose blood our red ensigns has not aspersed
But filled the goblets of their drunken lust.

Aye, we were stronger, we whose soul is wrought
Upon the fire and made with flame and ash,
Yet by the power of that One name the clash
They stayed of our invincible onslaught.

But now thy lightless eyes that overpass
The girdle of our vaster battle-field,
Shall break the charm of their enchanted shield
And pierce the strongest steel of their cuirass.

Henceforth thy word into the cannon bronze
We cast, our new commandments to proclaim;
Thou art the Vestal of the greatest flame,
Thou art the Sybil of the last response.

And when their Christ they conjure to condone
Their deeds of blood, our sins of love by thee
Shall be dispersed — a higher Calvary
Thou didst ascend to suffer and atone.

IV

And lo! As thou hast seen it, it shall be.
One day we shall relight our bivouac fires
Upon the embattled streets of our grandsires
And swear once more to die or to be free.

One day our bleeding, ever plodding feet,
Lit by the torch of love, shall stop before
The House of Greed, and hard upon the door,
Clenched in our fist the scythe of Time shall beat.

Two messengers that day shall pass the gate,
One, white-clad, who shall bear the salt and bread
Of peace, and One who cloaked in gory red
Shall bring the everlasting doom of hate.

Thou shalt be first, and say (for thou shalt live
Till then, thou who hast known no mortal sin):
"Your brother stands without, let him come in
And all your great misdeeds he will forgive.

"Your brother whom you cast away to roam
In misery and shame and toilsome woe,
Comes back in arms, and yet not like a foe,
But like a guest he will re-enter home.

"Open your door, receive him at your hearth,
Break bread with him and he shall break his sword,
And from this day the kingdom of the Lord
Be evermore established on the earth."

Thus shalt thou say. But if his heart of guilt
Be hardened, then the Somber One whose brow
Is seared by all the fires and ne'er did bow
Shall come forth, both his hands upon the hilt.

'Twill not be I, but one in whom my breath
Will pass before I die; for to my Dream
I ask no guerdon but this gift supreme,
The beauty of the battle and of death.

"Harken!" he'll say. "In vain we begged your dole,
For mercy, for the common bond of blood,
For love of man, for fear of your own god,
For the salvation of your deathless soul.

"We served you, fed you, housed you, cheered or wept
When you were glad or sad; when sick we nursed
You back to health; your foes we fought and cursed;
We watched your gold, we labored while you slept.

"We mourned your dead, we blessed your children's name,
We gave to you our sweat, our tears, our lives,

The virtue of our daughters and our wives,
Our share of heaven, our hoary, mothers' shame.

"Always unfelt, unseen, ununderstood,
Our love for you all suffered and forgave.
When you did strike us, we acclaimed you brave;
When you despised our lives, we hailed you good.

"Nothing we claimed and little did we beg;
Bereft of all, in famine, old, diseased,
After your dogs were filled, and when you pleased,
We asked to have the offal and the dreg.

"We only asked enough to live — not this,
Your life, but just to toil and not to die:
A loaf, a bed, a rag, a sheltered sty,
Your god to worship and your hand to kiss.

"No more we asked. But, lo, you heard us not,
You drove us from your kennels and you grinned
When in the cold, the snow, the rain, the wind,
You damned our souls to hell, our flesh to rot.

"You drove our babes to starve, the strong to drink,
The weak to beg, our famished girls to fill
The charnels of your stews, our sons to kill
For bread and work . . . and all of us to think!

"And so we thought. Behold the morning hour,
Your last, the crimson dawn that drives the fogs.
We have come back, not like a pack of dogs
That to new bones and an old whip will cower,

"Not like a drove of cattle which the knife
Can silence and the rope can yoke and bind,
But like the first vanguard of humankind
That comes into its heritage of life.

"We ask no more for work, for love, for bread.
We are the stronger now, we bring no peace.
Monster, your hour is struck, get on your knees,
We come not for your gold — we want your head!"

To the One Who Waits

No! whether a sob or a song,
    While love shall life's battles endure,
While you in my will shall be strong
    And I in your faith shall be pure,

While both have to weep, but our soul
    Knows not what is doubt or despair,
While happiness be not our goal,
    But simply the way to get there;

While after each loss we are trying
    Again, though we never achieve,
And, mocked at and wounded and dying,
    We still shall persist and believe,

While after each stormy nightfall
    More radiant each sunrise will seem,
And while, after having lost all,
    Remain you and I and the Dream —

Even though all the world shall adverse us,
    Though all our destruction acclaim
And priests in God's name shall accurse us,
    And fools in humanity's name;

Though all our old comrades we lose,
    And each of our friends turn a knave,
And some pull the hangman's red noose,
    And all help to dig us a grave,

Still this unto you will I tell,
    That no man, no scaffold, no jail,
No powers of heaven and hell
    Against you and me shall prevail!

OTHER POEMS

PROEM

My heart is a grim stronghold on a rock
Upon a tideless sea that no wind moves;
My hatreds in its oubliettes I lock
And from its walls I hang my faithless loves.

Around its ghostly towers gaunt vultures flock,
A red-eyed mastiff in its foul moat roves,
And black-cowled monks the nightlong curse and mock
The strangled dreams that mould in its alcoves.

Impregnable without as hell's own gate
Is from within, despair and rage combine
To make it dark and fierce and desolate;

From there I rule over a dead empire,
But in its cave I keep a cask of wine,
And in its belvedere a silver lyre.

"O LABOR OF AMERICA: HEARTBEAT OF MANKIND"

Come then, come now, sweat, sooty red-eyed, flame-scorched vestals of the eternal fire of steel
and coal and steam and wood, and stone and tools that make bread and surcease from want
and woe.

Human machines actioned by hope and ambition and oiled with blood, miners, stokers, ham-
mersmiths, builders, converters, puddlers, engineers of chasms, escalators and defiers of
the Babylon heights — O Labor of America, O heartbeat of Mankind,
Come before and beyond all authorities, rules, edicts, ukases, injunctions and excommunications
and foregather and proclaim yourselves in the great deed of Liberty.
For you have lightened the night of your dream even to the humbling of sunrise.

Welcome, dark, fierce cities, daughters of volcanoes, hearths and matrices of the new world —
Duquesne, Homestead, Calumet, Buffalo, sleepless and tortured and flint-faced.
And you, Braddock, fevered with an endless contemplation of the Satanic glow,
And you, Pueblo, titan-limbed, monster biceps bursting in the almighty effort of gestation and
agony of the implacable fecundity of our ferocious industry.

And you, McKeesport, mountain-ribbed, and you Akron and Youngstown, rubber-thewed, washing your stolid blank faces in your rusty creeks,

And you, astraddle the Styx and the Acheron, Pittsburgh, wrathful resting grave of spent meteors, gateway of Hell,

All ye, unhallowed grails of the last eucharist of sweat,

Welcome to the home of Labor, the last stricken Archangel,

For your resurrection has come.

Detroit has its hand on the lever, Gary maneuvers the brakes and Chicago, feeder of the world,

Rules the switches of the two-fisted earth.

If this is not the fullness of your glory, O American Labor, there is your New York, Cosmopolis of Mankind,

Whose towers you raised to mock the hurricanes and to shame and debase the clouds,

Whose harbor swallows the nations, whose people, myriad-tongued, absorb and reshape and amalgam all creeds, all races in one humanity.

Stand up, then, and take the earth unto your bosom,

Gather the oceans in your mighty cupped hands,

Cleanse the heavens of the scourges of the black demons

Of war, hate, fear and death and destruction,

Remold and reshape the soul of mankind

Into brave exploits of compassion and the dazzling splendor of reason and brotherhood.

Take most of our bread to the starving,

Whoever they be, wherever they be,

Fill your countless argosies with milk and honey

For the livid parched lips of the children

Of your erstwhile enemies and your detractors,

Uprise the fallen heroes, sustain the weak,

Comfort the widows the orphans and the bereft

Tear down the gateways to freedom to the imprisoned,

Turn the flood gates of light upon the entombed in darkness

Dry up the tears of shame and remorse

From the eyes of the harlot and the thief,

Smoothe the scowl of hate and revenge from the brow of the earth

And make of all her children the new, eternal united Israel of mankind.

And now we as Italian-Americans bow in both humility and pride as we ask you to stand by and acclaim your brothers from the land that gave a new hidden world to the world.

From that venerable mother of America, from the land of ecstasies and sorrows, of Ancient glories and unbearable humiliations,

From the garden of the earth, from the only land of many tender and mystic names: Etruria,
   Augusta, Enotria, Esperia, Saturnia, Vulcania, forever Italia, we call upon you to stop her
   weeping over earthquakes, eruptions and floods, and the desolation of ancient and new
   battlefields, to mingle with you in an everlasting embrace in amity and liberty and love.
Let our two nations, the Mother and her last Child march on together indissolubly until we
   weave forever
A shroud to all oppression
A bridal gown for the young earth,
Till we build together,
The city of the Sun,
The new Jerusalem,
The Peaceful House of Man.

New York and I

City without history and without legends,
City without scaffolds and without monuments,
Ruinless, shrineless, gateless, open to all wayfarers,
To all the carriers of dreams, to all the burden bearers,
To all the seekers for bread and power and forbidden ken;
City of the Common Men
Who work and eat and breed, without any other ambitions,
O Incorruptible Force, O Reality without visions,
What is between you and me?

You have narrowed my vast horizons
To the coil of your cold embrace,
You have shortened my star-girt heights
To the height of your bludgeoning mace;
You have pinioned my falcon flights
With the shears of your thieving measure,
You have seared my eyes with the sights
Of the stews where you rot and gloat;
You have parched my war-shouts in my throat
With the smudge of your hot bitumes,
You have choked my white prayers with the fumes
Of your toils and the dust of your streets.

In the charnels of my defeats,
In the welter of your foul trough
You have sealed in my lungs the cough
Of your sick and voracious breath;
You have poured the squalid death
Of your pleasures into my veins;
And all the things that are red,
And all the things that are vain.
What is between you and me, save the ashes and lees
Of orgies, the blows that you struck me, my impotent curse,
And now and again, in a fit of regret and remorse,
The truce of your soft lullaby, and my head on your knees?
I cursed in your temples, I wept leaden tears in your inns,
I laughed in your graveyards, I prayed in your slums for your blood,
I wallowed to purge my dead soul in the pools of your sins
And found the thing that's divine, the word that was God
In the filth of your offals and swill
That to your servants you fling,
When your law, when your fate and your will
Bade me to steal and to kill,
But the glory of your face made me sing!
And all the things that are dead
Tho' they were born to be deathlessly mine,
You have branded with kisses of fire on my flesh and my brain,
O Barren Harlot of heroes you turn into swine!

O Mad One, but how could I sing to you my last song?
O Dread One, how could I praise you, I who so long
Had seen you feed on the corpse of my dreams that you slew,
Gnaw at the plinths of all pillars I raised for the world,
Mock every flag I unfurled,
Rend every sail that I set and fell every oak that I grew?
How could I sing of you,
O Ferocious City who boils
All the mad powers of men in your cauldron, and stirs
Their molten furies with tridents of lust and despair
Till the flesh and the soul and the soil
Are turned into tinsel and coin for your dress and your hair?
What was between you and me, Grey City of Hunger and Toil?
But now . . . O Mighty One, what shiver shakes your form?
I see you awake and arisen,
Out of your golden seraglio, out of your lecherous prison,

Out of your shame and your sloth.
Naked your brow, your hair flung away to the breeze,
Naked your breasts, the wrath of the race in your knees,
Naked your sword, your gauntlet is cast on the seas,
And the breath of your shout swells the storm.
And shall you hear it now, the voice that smote behind
The locked gates of the past?
And shall you keep your troth?
And you will be steadfast?
And will you keep your promises or will they be refused
When rise to hail you mother the vanhosts of mankind?
Will then the blood you bleed and shed be re-transfused
Into fraternal veins? Will then the dead arise,
The starved be fed again, the sick again made whole?

And will you then have flowers to cover every tomb?
You who will slay the old world, will you then bear to light
Or crush within, the new one that stirs now, in your womb?
What matters all that now — now you have found a soul!
And lo! as now I hear you from sky and earth and water
Calling upon your children, to every son and daughter,
And tears are in your eyes, and in your hand is slaughter,
And you stand straight and terrible, cruel and holy, bruised
And blessed and bereft,
While stilled in your calm breast your every languish lies,
My heart has been unlocked, my silence has been cleft,
My song has been unloosed,
O Brazen One! O Dreadful One! O Glory of my eyes!

And so I shall sing with a song that shall bide in the ears
Of men, like the groan of the dying in those of the child,
All that in you is eternal and placid and wild,
All that is godlike or mean, till my light burns no more,
I shall sing your streets and your marts, many-tongued, myriad-armed,
Hallucinated with fires,
Athunder with tumult and roar;
Your human beehives alarmed
With frenzies of hates and desires:
I shall sing of your strong sons and weak ones,
The prophets and seers that you maim,
The singers you starve, the wastrels you fill,

The thieves and the strumpets you honor, the cowards you acclaim
And the saints and the heroes you kill.

I shall sing of your slums where you bleed,
Your machines, iron claws of your greed,
And your jails, viscid coils of your mind,
The light of your eyes that dazzles the sun
And turns your midnights into noons,
The Street where you buy and resell
Each day the whole world and mankind,
Your foundations that reach down to hell
And your towers that rend the typhoons,
And your voice drunk with bloody libations,
And your harbor that swallows the nations,
And the glory of your nameless dead,
And the bitterness of your bread,
And the sword that shall hallow your hand,
And the dawn that shall garland your head!

Spring in the Bronx Zoo

The trees are not yet full-burgeoned and not all the lawns are green
And only the self-made narcissus and the business-like dandelion (outriders and trumpeters of
     your chariot, O Primavera,)
Are up in the tremulous morn.
But most of the warm things are here, all stirring betimes,
For feather and hair are more punctual in April than petal and grass.
The tawny ducklings and cignets scratch through the silt of the pond
And shirr it behind them and throw it in shimmering folds on the banks.
The prairie puppies, the squirrelings sit up on their haunches,
The seal kids shiver and splutter hugging the rocks of the tanks
And the fledglings tumble like chestnut burrs down the branches.

The beavers paddle along hurriedly gnawing the reeds,
Felling the saplings, rebuilding again the old dam,
Not that the stream be unfriendly nor that the wind be unkind,
But because of an earth-old obedience to a task they shall never achieve.
Through the green bars of the den a kangaroo sticks her snout

To reach a tuft of pale moss and the pat of a timid hand;
And as from the slit of her pouch a startled young head peeps out:
"See?" shouts a child to its playmate, "Look at it now with your eyes!
I told you that babies aren't brought in by the storks and the doctors;
It is their mothers that grow them inside, and that's why they love them."
The other child stands bewildered, defeated, and thinks very hard
And turns his defeat to revolt, and he loses faith in his elders
And rises against all authorities, and he's grown up and set free.

The grey she-wolf leaves a trail of bluish milk in her tracks
As she runs and crouches and rears up the wooden pen where
Four slit black noses quiver and fume and sneeze in the sun.
Her jaws are a smouldering hearth, her eyes like dim candles
In quiet homes. She no longer lowers her head and recoils
When boys shout threats and insults to her who would croon like their mothers.
And the rouged girls do not giggle: "Whewff, why don't she take a bath,"
For though her odor is savage, it is not offensive but good
For she smells of fierce loves come to rest in the peace of motherhood
In the licking of her own blood and a new fear of life.

In her domed palace the lioness, opulent-haunched, golden-bellied,
Imperially lazy, voluptuous in her vain quest for hot sands,
An autonomous queen of the jungle caught in her time by a male,
Strides to and fro, to and fro, across her painted domain.
She roars not back to her consort, she hates him now, nor does she mind
His fierce alarums and boastings, as she lies down with great care.
She rasps with her dry purplish tongue her turgid pin teats looking round,
Dreaming and dreading and pleading and catching the eyes of the women,
Dreaming and wondering and fearing — for she is heavy with life.

But my goal in this last sanctuary of the lost world of my childhood,
(Are there left any worlds outside of children's books and young love,
And when shall we ever be wise if animals no longer speak?)
My goal is the cage of the big birds, the birds of prey and long flight,
The lonely ones, the star-sighted, cruel, admired and unloved.
Oh, when I look at the hawks staring at their useless talons,
At the owls blinking away the unfriendly sunshine from their eyes,
At the vultures drooping their heads, picking their breasts, in memory of the nipped storm
    clouds,
At the seagulls broken-winged, earth-ridden, their beaks turned up to the skies,
Would I could feed them instead of the meat of dead horses

The juicy hearts of ring doves
And the lying eyes of my loves
And the brains of our politicians,
The dried kidneys of our patricians
And the cowardly tongues of my senseless remorses.

The rest, the full-winged brood I love not in this place,
They like their cage, have a tree.
They mate in the ground, they have the comfort of song,
They fly and believe they are free.
The lark I love not who feeds on the buffalo's dung,
Nor the nightingale that was snatched from the cypresses of Italy
And died last week and was thrown in a garbage can,
Nor the thrush, nor the finch, nor the wren, nor the blue solitaire
From whom they stole even his proud loneliness,
Not even the swallow, first born of the earth and the air.
I only pity the condor who tears his own flesh in distress,
And love the red eagle who perches alone in his pen
Who no longer will challenge the sun, who no longer will soar,
This ever-awake, ever-silent, ever-unmoved emperor
Doomed to eat carrion and die in the coop of a hen.

Ah no! For when the hailstorm shall beat at last on these vaults,
This last archangel of all the heaven-shaking revolts
May yet crash down the white crags of his dream of the stars,
Beating his pinions between the red thunderbolts
And dashing his beak and his heart against the steel bars.

LITANY OF THE REVOLUTION

Prolétaires à cheval
— TROTSKY

Stand ho! the knighthood of the spade round up your madcap cavalcade, your ride is done, your spurs are won, dismount here on the accolade, here ends your first world-errantry.　　　　　　　　　　　　　　　　　*End of the Struggle*

Come around the liberty tree bastard willow, mongrel oak without nests and without shoots, dangling corpses are its fruits, twisted skeletons its roots; but　　*The Liberty Tree* though hacked and reft asunder by the axe and by the thunder, never ho! will it go under, it will never end in smoke.

Vault on your red-pennoned lance join the bivouac's wild dance, horse to horse and man to man throw aside your yataghan, muskets, holsters, bandoleers, sport it now as cavaliers, hug the buxom vivandieres, kiss and pinch the fat-haunched nurses and with laughter songs and curses boom the ribald jamboree.

The Merrymaking

Come around the liberty tree, hop pell-mell and romp and yell:

While we have a single shell for a master or a knave who won't work or won't rebel, war is heaven, peace is hell, let us dance the Tarantelle all around the liberty tree.

The Dances of the Revolution

La Tarantella

Come and kick up fast and hard La Gaillarde and kick up the roistering Braule, scramble in the dizzy whirls of the capering Rigadoon, beggar, poet, serf, buffoon, villain, craftsman, one and all, kitchen maids and scullion girls, bow along the staid Gavotte to the hurdy-gurdy tune!

La Gaillarde
The Brawl
Le Rigodon
La Gavotte

Come ye, jacques and sansculottes, come, black-stockinged Hebertists, Jacobins and Babouvists, chansonniers and pamphleteers, mad philosophers, grim sages, social quacks of all the ages; from the gutter and the rostrum, from the jail, the pauper's home, come with every salve and nostrum from the gospel to the bomb; come with tears and come with laughter, finders of new roads to Rome, harbingers of all hereafters, prophets of all kingdoms come; commissars and carbonaris, come and yowl your charivaris, shout once more your loud response to the tocsin's midnight call — round the lanthorn on the wall let us dance La Carmagnole to the music of the guns!

The Seers and the Doers

"Dansons la Carmagnole Vive le son du canon!"

Nearer nearer tears and grows through the tundras and the snows ever closer, closer, close the Cotillon grand finale to the flag-flame that has hurled like the dawn across the world l'Internationale!

Le Cotillon

L'Internationale

Come around its fiery graal that sears all the earth and scorches the Gilt Monster's face and hands, throw into its blaze your torches and your brands; midnight lamps and votive tallows, broken crosses and torn gallows, blow it with your song's fierce bellows, burn the whole world free!

Harken to the matins bells peal from every citadel where your souls were pent and crammed in the dungeons of despair, raise again the oriflammed gonfalon of Lucifer and intone your litany, the Magnificat of hell, the Te Deum of the damned, Man's first chant of victory.

Hail, O Creator, servant, dictator, hastener, waiter of all the things that are new!

The Litany

Peace that all seeds rears to flower and toil and truth are your power, com-

65

mand and eternate his hour, make time bow allegiance to you, now and forevermore.

Temple of peace and war, archway of love's main stream, altar where all men kneel down to adore themselves, only to find this law supreme that they who serve the most grasp life's best lore, stand by your unlocked door to bow in with each change a greater dream now and forevermore.

Revealment of our faith, achievement of our death, passion, conception, breath and tool of all our arts, what your stern rule imparts your mercy, being man-born, supersedes.

Sower of doubts and creeds, blower of thoughts and deeds, mower of all the harvests of our pain,

O flesh immortal, o eternal brain, bear, nurse, reward, sustain whoever has a gentle gift to bring, all those who toil and march, all those who sing, all those who stand true watch by your domain, and those also who dream and do nothing.

Today, tomorrow, till your next call ring, and then once more again.

Our Mother
the Revolution

Deliverer of doubters, deliverer of weaklings, deliverer of scoffers, deliverer from poverty and pelf, deliverer of each one from himself,

Blaster of every cell where men's souls grope (ambition, worry, hate, despair and hope).

Knight of the bad thief's cross,

Knight of the gibbet's rope knight of the fallen star, sealer of every tomb, healer of every womb and every scar.

Almoner of the poor, comforter of all grief, rich brother of the thief, chaste sister of the whore, messiah of the ultimate belief, alchemist who turns gold into manure;

Singer of love and arms, ringer of glad alarms, bringer of balms and charms that make flesh hard and eager to endure the stigmata of all your epopees,

Captain of phalanxes, assembler of cohorts for the unending sports of Labor's own gigantic holidays;

Beater of morning drums, stirrer of merrier laughs and holier sobs, pilot of every wing and every prow, ensign of all storm-riven labarums, antiphonary of all singing mobs,

Master, Redeemer, Comrade, Friend, come now!

The Liberator

The last
Knighthood

The least of
these

Come, O Truth, this is your hour, rise against the fates, the times, the place, the law, the multitude!

Stand and conquer, smite, devour every drowsy certitude, every reason, every sense that holds forth against your storm the dry logic of a norm and a palsied consuetude.

"Veni, Creator
Spiritus"

Self-engendering force, immense will, Inscrutable, Enorme, make us serve you stern and joyous and however you employ us, to upraise or to destroy us prove our faith in you and live!

For this glimpse of the eternal that you grant our blind belief, be it heavenly or infernal, for this last reprieve from error, for this mad escape from doubt be it permanent or brief, there's no scourge we won't bear out.

Loose upon us war and terror, livid famine, red-eyed drought; girt our homes with fire and slaughter, burn our fields, dry up our water, make black pestilence our warden, of each fruit tree in our garden make a gibbet and a stake; make our own blast tear and rend us, but be with us, O Tremendous, and keep us awake!

Spare or flay us, save or slay us, second ruler of the chaos, in this red Jehosaphot

Let us teem or let us rot, but first rip up, scotch and blot every root of the old weed that crushed out our hardest seed: ruler, master, conqueror, avatar and ancestor, monger, soldier, priest and judge, choke them with your thickest smudge, drown them in your foulest mire, blast them with your hottest fire, till nothing's left but your song, and your glory and your sorrow and the clean, wind-swept tomorrow naked, free and young!

O Revolution, voice of all things that are mute,
Our mother who art everywhere
All those who are about to live salute
Thee who will never die! All pure, all kind, the banners of your grace are up the wind over the ensanguined earth a rainbow manifold, crimson and green and gold, above the habitations of mankind flung out in the sweet air.

Let now your peace arise serene and fair like a clear morning call and like a prayer at eventide when every strength grows weak; and let your song that leaps from peak to peak be but the clarion charge of Work all-knowing, the hum of the machines, the joyous blowing of steamy throats of steel, the gentle lowing along the placid fields of plowing cattle; and lo! your shout of battle be now the hallelujah of rebirth!

O without fear, supreme fulfilled desire,
O ember everlive of the first fire,
O love eternal, o eternal mirth, replenish now the bare arms of the earth with a new race of men

Ready to fight but readier yet to serve, a sacred urn each one there to preserve till you return again a splurting fuse to your almighty bolt.

Engender with each law its twin revolt,
Mother, Redeemer, Comrade, Friend! AMEN!

The Lost Leader

He too is gone. Yet he was strong and brave
Like those who all have staked and sacrificed
As they marched forth to their own nameless grave
Forgotten even by the cross of Christ.

Like the couriers who bear up to the gate
Of life the challenge of their flags unfurled,
And their death sentence and the mob's mandate
And the first stone to cast at the old world.

The greater love that all our hatred hallows
No nobler heart than his shall ever embrace;
He fought with us, with us he dared the gallows,
And hunger and derision and disgrace,

And the supreme insult of his own doubt;
And when defeat waylaid him with a lie,
And hope lay crushed stampeded in the rout,
And all was lost except the will to die,

He built with the black ruins of disaster
A sacrificial altar to his soul,
For hope is vast, but courage is much vaster
When death, not victory is the farther goal.

Yet, neither want made him adore the beast,
Nor lure of gold bade him forget his word,
Nor the black curse of a blaspheming priest,
Nor kingly favors, nor the soldier's sword;

He stood by us when love and fame and glory
Beckoned away from where our struggles led . . .
And left us — oh the shame of the vile story! —
      Just for a harlot's bed.

WHEN THE GREAT DAY CAME

On the Anniversary of the Russian Revolution

In the beginning was the Thought, and the Thought was with Man, and the Thought was Man.

The same was in the beginning, before there was either god or law or the promise of things to be;

And life was the shadow of Man cast upon the land and the water by the light of Thought,

And death the defeated desire to lift that shadow onto the stars.

Now all the great beginnings engender two things, one male and one female, and so with Thought, which begat two things, and one was the Deed, which was male, and one the Ideal which was female.

And the Deed dwelled alone with himself and grew fierce and mighty and invincible, save by life which is multitude,

And the Ideal went forth to all things and grew weaker as it expanded, and easy to conquer, save by death which is solitude,

And the Deed became a sword, and the Ideal became a cross,

And lo! there was strife between them, and the Deed prevailed always, until the prophecy was fulfilled.

Now this was the prophecy which was heard rising out of the tumult and wailing of nations, out of the roar of the splitting chaos,

Saying: When she who is twirling the spindle and swaying the loom shall go forth into the fields and goad the oxen and push the plow in the furrow;

And she who is washing the wounds of the warriors with the salve of her silent tears, shall seize a sword and wield it like a man,

Then will the great day come.

And when he who rides the earth astride his black stallion shall dismount by the well and bemoan the hardness of the road;

And he who now gores the heifers and hacks the fruit trees in bloom shall seek the peace of his fury and knit by the hearth;

And he who warms his hairy hands in the entrails of his foe shall croon a lullaby and rock a cradle at dusk,

Then will the Spokesman return, then the Ideal will triumph and the Deed become her manservant forever,

Then will the great day come.

And lo! as the prophecy spake, so it came to pass, after a million years, after a thousand doctrines, after a hundred gods,

Yea, even after the great flood of blood, in the least of all nations, as it was foretold.

For the man who measured the earth by the length of his knout is fallen from his chariot and babbles a prayer in the dust,

And his crown which outshone the sun now lies on the floor of the earth, a toy for the peasant's child,

And his charger which trampled the nations is now harnessed onto a dungcart,

And his mastiff which tore the flesh of the saints now leads the steps of a blind beggar;

And the hut of the hermit is now too large for him who held a province too small for his kennels,

And a loaf of black bread is dearer to him now than a mountain of gold;

For the People have got together,

For the People have got together and have risen,

For the People have got together and shattered his throne!

And behold! The woman hath risen and rent her garment of mourning and she hath shaken the dust from her knees and vested the armour,

She hath broken her distaff and made a spear, she hath torn the bandage from her wounds and made a red pennant in the fray,

She hath blown out the lamps of the temple and kindled a fire on the hill and set a torch by the sea;

And her mouth which was stuffed with ashes and prayers now shouts fierce orders to the storm.

Behold! Her hands have gathered in sheaves the white arrows of the thunder

And she sits no longer on the threshold dreading the return of her sons,

No longer she prays in the night for the peace of the dead, nor does she rise in the dark to propitiate the cruel daybreak with her brow on the hearthstone.

But she stands rigid and naked, most dreadful and beauteous to behold,

In the noonday of the world, upon the ramparts of time,

Calling, calling, calling,

Calling to the east and the west, calling to the north and the south,

Calling to the white man and the yellow man and the black man with the wild shouts of her mouth

To rise and stand up together,

To rise and stand up together against nature and destiny,

To rise and stand up together in one holy fraternity,

To rise and conquer the earth

With labor and love and mirth,

One race, one tongue, one birth,

One dream of eternity.

WHEN THE COCK CROWS

To the memory of Frank Little hanged at Midnight

I

Six men drove up to his house at midnight, and woke the poor woman who kept it,

And asked her: "Where is the man who spoke against war and insulted the army?"

And the old woman took fear of the men and the hour, and showed them the room where he slept,

And when they made sure it was he whom they wanted, they dragged him out of his bed with blows, tho' he was willing to walk,

And they fastened his hands on his back, and they drove him across the black night,

And there was no moon and no star and not any visible thing, and even the faces of the men were eaten with the leprosy of the dark, for they were masked with black shame,

And nothing showed in the gloom save the glow of his eyes and the flame of his soul that scorched the face of Death.

II

No one gave witness of what they did to him, after they took him away, until a dog barked at his corpse.

But I know, for I have seen masked men with the rope, and the eyeless things that howl against the sun, and I have ridden beside the hangman at midnight.

They kicked him, they cursed him, they pushed him, they spat on his cheeks and his brow,

They stabbed his ears with foul oaths, they smeared his clean face with the pus of their ulcerous words,

And nobody saw or heard them. But I call you to witness, John Brown, I call you to witness, you Molly Maguires,

And you, Albert Parsons, George Engle, Adolph Fischer, August Spies,

And you, Leo Frank, kinsman of Jesus, and you, Joe Hill, twice my germane in the rage of the song and the fray,

And all of you, sun-dark brothers, and all of you harriers of torpid faiths, hasteners of the great day, propitiators of the holy deed,

I call you all to the bar of the dawn to give witness if this is not what they do in America when they wake up men at midnight to hang them until they're dead.

III

Under a railroad trestle, under the heart-rib of progress, they circled his neck with the noose, but never a word he spoke.

Never a word he uttered, and they grew weak from his silence,
For the terror of death is strongest upon the men with the rope,
When he who must hang breathes neither a prayer nor a curse,
Nor speaks any word, nor looks around, nor does anything save to chew his bit of tobacco and
    yawn with unsated sleep.
They grew afraid of the hidden moon and the stars, they grew afraid of the wind that held its
    breath, and of the living things that never stirred in their sleep,
And they gurgled a bargain to him from under their masks.
I know what they promised to him, for I have heard thrice the bargains that hounds yelp to the
    trapped lion:
They asked him to promise that he would turn back from his road, that he would eat carrion as
    they, that he would lap the leash for the sake of the offals, as they — and thus he would
    save his life.
But not one lone word he answered — he only chewed his bit of tobacco in silent contempt.

IV

Now black as their faces became whatever had been white inside of the six men, even to their
    mothers' milk,
And they inflicted on him the final shame, and ordered that he should kiss the flag.
They always make bounden men kiss the flag in America where men never kiss men, not even
    when they march forth to die.
But tho' to him all flags are holy that men fight for and death hallows,
He did not kiss it — I swear it by the one that shall wrap my body.
He did not kiss it, and they trampled upon him in their frenzy that had no retreat save the rope,
And to him who was ready to die for a light he would never see shine, they said, "You are a coward."
To him who would not barter a meaningless word for his life, they said, "You are a traitor."
And they drew the noose round his neck, and they pulled him up to the trestle, and they
    watched him until he was dead,
Six masked men whose faces were eaten with the cancer of the dark,
One for each steeple of thy temple, O Labor.

V

Now he is dead, but now that he is dead is the door of your dungeon faster, O money changers
    and scribes, and priests and masters of slaves?
Are men now readier to die for you without asking the wherefore of the slaughter?
Shall now the pent-up spirit no longer connive with the sun against your midnight?
And are we now all reconciled to your rule, and are you safer and we humbler, and is the night
    eternal and the day forever blotted out of the skies,

And all blind yesterdays risen, and all tomorrows entombed,
Because of six faceless men and ten feet of rope and one corpse dangling unseen in the blackness under a railroad trestle?
No, I say, No. It swings like a terrible pendulum that shall soon ring out a mad tocsin and call the red cock to the crowing.
No, I say, No, for someone will bear witness of this to the dawn,
Someone will stand straight and fearless tomorrow between the armed hosts of your slaves, and shout to them the challenge of that silence you could not break.

VI

"Brothers" — he will shout to them — "are you, then, the God-born reduced to a mute of dogs
That you will rush to the hunt of your kin at the blowing of a horn?
Brothers, have then the centuries that created new suns in the heavens, gouged out the eyes of your soul,
That you should wallow in your blood like swine,
That you should squirm like rats in a carrion,
That you, who astonished the eagles, should beat blindly about the night of murder like bats?
Are you, Brothers, who were meant to scale the stars, to crouch forever before a footstool,
And listen forever to one word of shame and subjection,
And leave the plough in the furrow, the trowel on the wall, the hammer on the anvil and the heart of the race on the knees of screaming women, and the future of the race in the hands of babbling children,
And yoke on your shoulders the halter of hatred and fury,
And dash head-down against the bastions of folly,
Because a colored cloth waves in the air, because a drum beats in the street,
Because six men have promised you a piece of ribbon on your coat, a carved tablet on a wall and your name in a list bordered with black?
Shall you, then, be forever the stewards of death, when life waits for you like a bride?
Ah no, Brothers, not for this did our mothers shriek with pain and delight when we tore their flanks with our first cry;
Not for this were we given command of the beasts,
Not with blood but with sweat were we bidden to achieve our salvation.
Behold: I announce now to you great tidings of joy,
For if your hands that are gathered in sheaves for the sickle of war unite as a bouquet of flowers between the warm breasts of peace,
Freedom will come without any blows save the hammers on the chains of your wrists and the picks on the walls of your jails!
Arise, and against every hand jeweled with the rubies of murder,
Against every mouth that sneers at the tears of mercy,
Against every foul smell of the earth,

Against every hand that a footstool raised over your head,
Against every word that was written before this was said,
Against every happiness that never knew sorrow,
Arid every glory that never knew love and sweat,
Against silence and death, and fear,
Arise with a mighty roar!
Arise and declare your war:
For the wind of the dawn is blowing,
For the eyes of the East are glowing,
For the lark is up and the cock is crowing,
And the day of judgment is here!"

VII

Thus shall he speak to the great parliament of the dawn, the witness of this murderous midnight,
And even if none listens to him, I shall be there and acclaim,
And even if they tear him to shreds, I shall be there to confess him before your guns and your gallows, O Monsters!
And even tho' you smite me with your bludgeon upon my head,
And curse me and call me foul names, and spit on my face and on my bare hands,
I swear that when the cock crows I shall not deny him.
And even if the power of your lie be so strong that my own mother curse me as a traitor with her hands clutched over her old breasts,
And my daughters with the almighty names, turn their faces from me and call me coward,
And the One whose love for me is a battleflag in the storm, scream for the shame of me and adjure my name,
I swear that when the cock crows I shall not deny him.
And if you chain me and drag me before the Beast that guards the seals of your power, and the caitiff that conspires against the daylight demand my death,
And your hangman throw a black cowl over my head and tie a noose around my neck,
And the black ghoul that pastures on the graves of the saints dig its snout into my soul and howl the terrors of the everlasting beyond in my ears,
Even then, when the cock crows, I swear I shall not deny him.
And if you spring the trap under my feet and hurl me into the gloom, and in the revelation of that instant eternal a voice shriek madly to me
That the rope is forever unbreakable,
That the dawn is never to blaze,
That the night is forever invincible,
Even then, even then, O Monsters, I shall not deny him.

THE DAY OF WAR

A Hawk-faced youth with rapacious eyes, standing on a shaky chair,
Speaks hotly in the roar of the crossways, under the tower that challenges the skies, terrible like
    a brandished sword.
A thin crowd, idle, yawning, many-hungered, beggarly-rich
With the heavy booty of the hours of dreaming and scheming,
Imperial ruins of the mob,
Listens to him wondering why he speaks and why they listen.
The fierce incandescence of noon quivers and drones with the echoes
Of distant clamors, grumbling of voices, blaring of speed-mad fanfares,
Of suddenly drowned outcries.
But as the roar reaches the group, it turns and recoils and deviates,
And runs around it as a stream runs round a great rock.
Stirred by the blue fans of the skies his black hair is caught and entangled in a little cloud
    between the tall roofs
And only his voice is heard in the little island of silence.
His arms go up as he speaks; his white teeth fight savagely with his black eyes,
His red tie flies tempestuously in the wind, the unfurled banner of his heart amidst the mus-
    ketry of his young words.
He has been speaking since dawn; he has emerged from the night, and the night alone shall sub-
    merge him.
They listen to him and wonder, and grope blindly in the maze of his words;
They fear his youth and they pity it;
But the sunshine is strong on his head,
And his shadow is heavy upon their faces.
Suddenly, like a flash of yellow flame,
The blast of a trumpet shoots by, smiting the white tower like a hail of gold coins.
The soldiers march . . . Tramp, tramp, tramp . . . The soldiers march up the avenue.
And lo! the crowd breaks, scatters, runs away,
And only six listeners remain:
A girl, a newsboy, a drunken man, a Greek who sells rugs, an old man and the stranger I know.
But he speaks on, louder, with the certainty of the thunder that only speaks after the bolt.
"Workers of America, we alone shall acquit this generation before history. We must and shall
    stop this war."
Tramp, tramp, tramp — the soldiers are marching . . .
The Greek vendor moves on; wearily the old man turns towards a seat, far away in the rustling
    park.
But he speaks on.
"The great voice of labor shall rise fearlessly today, and the world shall listen, and eternity shall
    record his words."
Tramp, tramp, tramp — the soldiers march near by.

The drunken man grumbles, stares at his open hands and lurches away towards an approaching car.

But he speaks on.

"Our protest and our anger will be like a cloudburst, and the masters will tremble. Brothers, don't you see it? The revolution is at the threshold."

The newsboy swings his bag over his shoulders, and dashes away through the park.

But he speaks on.

"As sure as this sun shall set, so will tyranny go down. Men and women of America, I know that the great day is come!"

Tramp, tramp, tramp — the soldiers sing as they march!

The stranger I know shrinks in the hollow places of himself, he fades and vanishes, molten in the heat of that young faith.

But the girl stands still and immovable, her upturned face glowing before the brazier of his soul,

As from the tower drop one by one at his feet the twelve tolls of the clock that marks time, the time that flows and flows on until his day comes . . .

And the girl and the tower and he

Are the only three things that stand straight and rigid and inexpugnable

Amidst the red omens of war,

In the fullness of the day,

In the whiteness of the moonlight,

In the city of dread and uproar.

One Against the World

They said: Leave the plow in the furrow, leave the pruning hook in the bleeding branch awaiting the virgin vigor of the graft; leave the hammer on the anvil; leave the saw on the plank, the awl on the last, the needle in the cloth, the bobbin in the loom, the trowel by the wall, leave the unfinished task of peace and welfare and love for the joy and promise of all men, and go to war, sturdy lad, go to war. Your country needs you.

They said again: Leave open the book over which the dim lamp watched the first vigils of your spirit and your mind; leave the lancet which sought in the dead flesh the quiver of life, the rudder that guided the ship to the infinitudes, the telescope which disclosed to your mortal gaze the lanes of the stars and the glorious mystery of the sun. Leave the humble quill on the unwritten page, the brush on the pallette, the bow on the string, the chisel on the marble — banish your thoughts, strangle the anxiety of your soul, forswear and despise everything that distinguished you, a man, from the beast, and go to war, stalwart youth. Your country calls you.

And again they said: Leave your mother who has borne you in great pain and nursed you with the milk of her breast, the mother of whom you were the only glory and her greatest happiness; eschew your old father who gave for you his scant bread and the sweat of his brow; foresake your brothers who expected protection and guidance; and abandon also the One who destiny set upon your road, the One who saw all her life in your eyes, in the roseate dream of her innocent heart. Choke the cry of your entrails, smother the breath of your soul, swallow the sobs that rise in your throat, conceal as a cowardice and an infamy the tears that dim your eyes, and go to war, mighty youth. Your country wants you.

And they said other things, weird and terrible and most stupefying, but all cruel things, and no one was surprised, and no one discussed and reasoned them out, because they were ancient and immemorable things which had been said since the beginning of the world, and down the endless chain of eons they had been harkened and accepted without thought or protest. And so from eras to centuries, and from centuries to years, and from years to days, all went meekly to war.

And the Lawgiver said: It is necessary;
The Magistrate said: It is dutiful.
The Philosopher said: It is human.
The Scientist said: It is natural.
The Artist said: It is beautiful.
The Poet said: It is glorious.
The Priest said: It is divine.

Only one rose among so many and said:
It is not just.

And all turned against him, and they insulted him, and beat him and hanged him and said: He Is Mad.

PAGAN SPRING

Beloved, Mid-March is here again, the day I have saved for my gods
(I know that one day they'll return), and for the confession of me
Before all the things that are humble: the flowers, the waters, the clouds
And for the praise of springtime and the worship of Italy.

For tho' I have given America a whole youth of hours and days,
And tho' I have all but forgotten the spell and the lore of my land,

This day my heart, a red eagle sated with flights and big preys,
Trembles like a young fledgeling caught in the warmth of her hand.

And what if this song is disloyal to other songs that I sing?
What if I leave my new comrades one day for my ancient forbears?
Beloved, once in the year it is a permissible thing
To grow insane with the dreams of our unlived yesteryears.

And so I arose with the dawn, as by the sacred old rite
And watched for the rooks that the cock crows out of the blue glen,
And when the first lark went up, I bowed like the acolyte
And after each pause in their singing I humbly answered amen.

I went to the source by the hill to drink the earth-milk in the hollow
Of my cupped hands, and I washed the sleep off my eyes with the dew,
I turned down my quiver and each arrow became a wild swallow
And when the yearling colts neighed I dashed with them to meet you.

How holy the mountains looked bowing before the tall clouds
How frightened the chaste young streams awaking to puberty;
How wondrous the trees regathered in solemnly waiting crowds,
How patient the rivers still working full time for the wise old sea.

I saw the olives black-hooded, white-cowled like old monks, chanting
The matins, exhorting the vaporing plains and the mist-blue hills.
I saw the feast garmented almonds scolding the orchards and granting
A nod to the rival gardens and a broad grin to the sills.

I heard again the old belfry awakening the flock of red roofs
To smoke and sparks, and the rattle of buckets and chains in the wells,
I heard the dogs yawning, the clanking of harness, the stamping of hoofs
And the smith's hammer resuming its quarrelsome brawl with the bells.

I heard the wind rustle through the ever-awake cypresses
And through the bays ever-dreaming, and over the palaces — and
Holding at once its chilled breath and hushing with sudden distress
As it passed over the tombs with wings folded over its head.

I saw him raise up the meadows like mighty hosts in swift marches,
Soothe the stone faces of heroes and heal the wounds and the scars
Of broken statues, and ruins of temples and bridges and arches
Embalmed with pollens and mosses and dust of the fallen stars.

At the Prayer Meeting

Now that I heard them all, the pure, the meek,
The learned and the patient and the wise,
And him who gives and him who does not seek,

And him who chastened both his hands and eyes,
And him who moans his woes and his disgrace,
And him who serves, a king in mean disguise;

O Lord, I climb onto the highest place,
And even as the ancient Pharisee,
I lift my voice now steep into thy grace.

I thank thee, Lord, that I am not as he
Who humbles thine fierce image in the dust
And thinks that by his shame he honors thee,

And I give praise that I am far more just
Than yonder fool, who in his heart has slain
All thy great gifts, his passions and his lust,

And the diviner appetites for pain,
And said in his fool heart that they who crave
The least shall hoard the fullest of their gain.

I coveted, instead, all things that gave
Thy law the sword, and to thy mercy boon,
The things thy justice smote but love forgave,

Lest I be even as thyself, and soon
Thy mighty name be blotted from the land,
And thy word be the jest of the buffoon.

I never raised against my friend my hand,
Nor to my dog my foot — but to my foe
Devoutly disregarding thy command,

I turned no cheek, but rendered blow for blow;
Unto no stranger lost thy ways I showed,
I fed no hungry ones, I did not go

With him who would me tread the righteous road
I visited no prisoners, I taught
No child, I lifted not my brother's load.

The widows and the orphans I forgot,
And lest my pity overreach on thine,
I left the sick to die, the dead to rot,

I craved all things unholy, that divine
They might be made by thine omnipotence;
I filled with flesh unclean, got drunk with wine,

I took what I must needs without pretence,
Was faithful to no master's trust and store
And paid not Caesar's tax, nor Peter's pence.

I shunned the wiseman's counsel and his lore,
I spurned the righteous, I despised the saint,
I traded with the thief and with the whore.

Yet sought I truth always, nor lie nor feint
I used to win, nor did the spirit wrong,
Nor of my wounds I ever made complaint.

Aye, and when beauty passed me by along
The road astrewn with all my broken dreams,
And hunger choked into my throat my song;

When to mine eyes the hidden world that seems
The foregloom of thy reddest hell unrolled
And filled mine ears with madmen's cries and screams;

When I saw justice prostrate, and revolt
Accursed, and thy cross smitten with the sword,
And knew that thou hadst lost thy thunderbolt,

I bade men rise, and thus I saved thy word,
I bade them strike, and thus upheld thy rule!
For this I thank thee, that I'm not, O Lord,

A liar and a knave like yonder fool!

The Bankrupt's Suicide

He lay in the silver-and-blue boudoir in the royal suite of the great hotel, full-stretched on the shimmering rug, a thin asp of black blood creeping down from his left nostril; his big hands open, giving back everything — his dream, his gold and his gun.

He had played the game manfully and fiercely and he had lost; and now he lay there as a last payment in full to the little mob that had come to cash his promise.

And the little mob that had been bought free by the blood of fools and had taken alms from the hands of beggars, waited for the scavenger of the law to turn out the pockets of this last monger of salvations who has failed for ten million dollars.

They glowered at him, their faces as vile with anger and as red as the buttocks of mandrills — choked with a sullen fury against death that had cheated them of their revenge;

Yet were he alive, could he but rise again, they would grovel before him and still acclaim the magic of his words and still pray that the alchemy of his brain turn their inanity into gold, their cowardice into power.

The painted ladies, the lawyers, the doctors, the divines, the God-fearing savers of money (savers of courage, savers of love, savers of laughter and expensive tears) jeered at him and cursed him mutely in their rage made righteous by the drunken nod of the law;

And one gnome shook his fist at him, and a braver one covered himself with glory by kicking the soles of his feet (he swerved his foot in time from the lean jaw of the dead for fear of the terror of the lightning still unspent in his eyes and the thunder still growling in his mouth).

And they all mouthed strange curses, invoking strange powers of wrath harrying God and the Devil with drooling incantations, ignobly defeated, guideless without him, and his corpse became for them the visible body of all life.

But before him, straight like a soldier standing at attention, a workman stood up with a pick grounded between his feet, presenting arms. He had failed a thousand times and was trying again; and now he mourned in this dead enemy a wayward comrade.

Te Deum of Labor

To thee whose rule of sweat and strife
Is like the sun's impassive course,
Eternal principle of life,
Instinct and will, idea and force,

Essence of each created thing,
Breath of all things that are to be,
God Labor, what we cannot sing
Let our hands do in praise to thee.

Thy law is just, thy burden light,
Thy grace the sole reward we ask,
To serve thee is a freeman's right,
To obey thee a lordly task,

For all are godlike who fulfill
Thy least desire, thy hardest rule,
And, brain or hand, obey thy will
With an old thought, with a new tool.

Thine everlasting toil combines
All that is good and true and fair;
The sooty demons in the mines,
The grim archangels in the air,

And those who wreathe thy brow with roses
Or wash thy feet have but one goal;
Damnation or apotheosis,
Thou art the measure of our soul.

At thy command the typhoons bow
And pull thy argosies in tow,
When thy strong arms bear down the plough
The deserts bloom, the harvests grow;

If thou stalk'st forth, the mountains quake,
Thou sigh'st, and storms attend thy breath,
And when thou sleep'st nothing's awake
Not even love, not even death.

Volcanoes drink from thy cupped hand
And cough their wrath in thy brass coils,
The bridled oceans through dry land
Follow thy finger to new toils,

And when across the skies and seas
Cleaves lightning-like thy trackless lane,
Thou linkest the eternities
From Jason's ship to Lindbergh's plane.

What shall we say, what shall we do
To make thy glory more sublime?
Thy godhead which is in us too
Stands both before and after time;

All things exist because thou art
Because of thee all things are fair
Abide then in our templed heart
And let thy will be this, our prayer:

Our father Labor stern and kind
Who art wherever life hath birth,
Thy will be done among mankind,
Come thy republic on the earth;

Give us this day our daily bread
Our daily task, our daily song,
Deliver us from all bloodshed
From greed and hate, from right and wrong,

Save us from envy and discord,
And when our day is done and when
Thy final whistle blows, O Lord,
Spare us the fear of death. Amen.

Anniversary I

Along the flocks of clouds that browse the firs
The moon goes like a mystic grail of light,
Between the bowed heads of the worshippers.

The branches of the oaks swing with a flight
Of censers and the poplars sing a psalm
Of ancient glory to the holy night.

Peace lies upon our roof, and in my palm
Your hand unclasped lies restful and secure,
And everything is strong and white and calm,

For we are still in love and are still poor.

Anniversary II

Three years we gnawed the bitter bread of war,
And now that peace is back from its vain quest,
The same mute beggar saints crowd up our door.

Come, Father Cold, sit by our hearth and rest;
Here, Sister Sickness, lie down on our bed;
Old Brother Hunger, be our honored guest.

Tomorrow all around the world shall spread
The tables of our feast, after this wake.
Tonight let us sit up and mourn our dead

For Russia and John Reed and Jesus' sake.

Anniversary III

Athwart life's last and broadest avenue
We raised as a triumphal arch our love,
And as the veteran years pass marching through,
It grows more stately old, more nobly true,
And though it crumbles down, it does not move.

Anniversary IV

When dusk prolongs the agony of light
On the bowed hills, and prostrate shadows creep
Up the pavillioned stairway of the night;

When nothing is awake or dares to sleep
For fear of death, save love that broods and stares,
And clouds hold back their rain, and you can't weep;

If I but catch your eyes and unawares
Your lips twitch with the sobs of our lost years,
Your smile then opens like the book of prayers

In which my mother kept her secret tears.

Anniversary V

Three times blared forth the clarion of the sun,
His stallions neighed and trampled on the roofs
His crimson mantle as he galloped on.

Upon the lawn mad March had left new proofs
Of his most ancient sorcery, for there lay
Amidst the tracks of faun and centaur hoofs

The spoor of a new man on a new way.
And lo! across the cannon smoke that arched
The dawn, loaded with gifts for the great day.

Springtime and love and revolution marched.

ANNIVERSARY VI

The flag says to the wind amidst the green
Of oaks and beeches as the curious sky
Leans down to listen: "What is there between

You and me, despot, that I droop and fly
At every whim of your mad heart?" And he
Who never answers save with a deep sigh:

"There are the ancient lore and destiny
Of tides and clouds that have obeyed my breath
Long ere you came, and made the law." — Thus be

With you, love, who came after song and death.

THE SENATE OF THE DEAD

I

When all was accomplished, the last Courier of the living met the Ambassador of the dead.
It was on a vast, grey meadow, and the great oaks towered in the distance, unstirred,
And thereunder, in the calm of the ages that rest, and the silence of the ages that wait, sat the
solemn assizes of the dead.
Mighty as if hewn by the bolt from a mountain of the earth to be a signal reef in the sea, and
armored with beaten steel, and bare in the legs, and bearded like a rock surrounded by
black pines, was the Ambassador of the dead.

And short like a mortar that fires rockets in the storm, and slim-limbed like the runners who bear fierce tidings was the Courier of the living who had come from afar with the crimson passports of his wounds and the flaming credentials of glory.

Said the gigantic gatekeeper: "Who art thou, and what seek'st thou here? Peace? 'Tis not here, for this is not the goal, but just a longer stop on the way."

And the Courier of the living answered him quietly, as men answer a fellow wayfarer about the road and the wherefore of their journey:

"My name is Karl Liebknecht, and I am from Germany, and I seek to see the faces of my comrades."

"Then come with me," spoke the great shade, and put his arm about the Newcomer, and they walked across the grey grass that closed behind them untrampled.

And the Newcomer discoursed with him graciously, unawed, equal to him, as strangers do when they talk ere they know each other.

II

Said the one heavy in armor, whose brown legs were wound with the latchet of the caliga and who bore upon his shoulder the great aegis of Greece,

Said he to the Newcomer: "I have been waiting for thee for twenty times one hundred years, ever since we, who were to die, sent the call of freedom to thy people.

They came, tall and white and blond, the axe-bearers of the North, and with them we swore an oath on the volcano, by the sacred hearth of the earth, that we should all be free or all die.

And now thou shalt meet them dead, the tall slaves of Germany with whom we defeated the legions in Lucania and Matapontus, and with whom I fell, each on his own sword, all freed of life, the great forger of chains. But tell me, are they free now, the living of thy land?"

The Newcomer looked deep into the sunken black eyes and answered: "Nay, not yet, but they soon shall be, for the bugles were still blowing, and it was still daylight when I left them. But who art thou, Captain, and wherefore dost thou embrace me, a hater of war?"

The Warrior kissed him on both cheeks and said: "Call me not captain, for I became a warrior out of the weariness of war. Call me comrade. My name is Spartacus."

And they walked along combing the silent grass with their feet, and the Thracian spoke of the first red dawn and the glory of the first uprising, and the great humiliation of Rome.

III

Another shade met them on the way; huge, gaunt, ungainly — a mighty column built up with the ruins of all the triumphal arches of the ages;

And he also put his arm about the Newcomer, and bent toward him, and his short black beard, still fragrant with the young winds of the prairies, brushed against the smooth cheek of the Newcomer, as he whispered:

"I knew of you, and I knew you would come, too. Years and years before you were born, I was told of you by the men of your country, who helped me to clean out the shame of my own.

You will meet them all here, but though they are dressed in blue, and wear brass buttons and medals and sabers, don't be shy of them, for they were regular fellows, not professional swashbucklers. We hadn't learned at that time to fight in overalls for liberty.

They came from Germany seeking freedom, and they brought a lot of it with them. But, say, are they free of their lords now? Do the people rule there?"

The Newcomer rested his head under the armpit of the big man and answered: "Not yet, but the Beast has been driven out of its lair, and the banners of the people are hoist beside the cross on the tall steeples. Lead me to my brothers, Master."

The smile broadened on the thick lips of the second shade. "Don't call me master, for I never taught anybody anything over there. Call me Abe, for that is my name, Abraham Lincoln. I wouldn't be surprised if you had heard of me."

And as they proceeded, the commoner held him close to his heart, father-like, and laughed and chuckled quietly, happily.

IV

Then, as they drew nearer to the great oaks, above which was neither light nor darkness, nor stars nor clouds, but the infinite unencompassed even by color,

Another came forth, whose face was white with the passion of bounden speech.

And the Newcomer saw him, and rushed to him, and they were locked in each other's arms, and the silence of the holy place grew deeper because of the thousands of ears that listened.

"Father," cried the Newcomer, "Oh Father, I have come as you said; I have been true to your legacy, and died where you bade me remain, poor and hunted, and cursed and defeated, but not shamed.

But it was not the monster that defeated me, Father; it was your comrades of yesterday, they who polluted the earth with the stench of their treason,

They who tore down the old ikons from their niches but held the foul temple still sacred,

They who made of Liberty an ignoble mouthing of vulgar words and of Revolution a mere exchange of seats and clothes!

But I fought them, Father, I fought them with your words and my own bare hands, and the night is not yet, for the cannon still roared when I came."

Their tears mingled as they embraced tighter, the tears of strong men, most dreaded force loosened upon the world,

And the Old Man murmured as he kissed him upon the back of the head: "My boy . . . my son . . . ," and could say no more.

But the Commoner understood, for he had held a whole race of men on his knees, and he chuckled louder, tho' his hand was spread tight on his face.

V

And now they were before the Silent Assembly that sat pleasantly under the oaks — thousands
  of men and women, serene and undisturbed;

And more of them came forth, and surrounded the Newcomer, and asked him what news he
  bore.

And among them was a frail, little woman, with shaggy hair and the beauty of the ravaged earth
  stamped upon her wan face;

And she also kissed him and said to her companions: "I shall introduce him, and you shall intro-
  duce the other, when she arrives. Yea, this is my privilege, for he did in Berlin when he
  died what I did in Paris on the day he was born."

The Newcomer stared at her mutely, and she understood his silent question and said: "They
  used to call me the Red Virgin, but I have borne thousands of children, and you are my
  best beloved. Don't call me comrade, call me mother. I tore down the Column Vendome
  and set the torch and the petrol to the Elysée, but it was not to destroy, but to give more
  light to the feet of the people. My name is . . ."

But before she said it, he seized her hands that looked like withered lilies, her hands that had
  lighted all the lamps on all the altars of love.

And he kissed upon their palms the stigmata of his own faith as he babbled like a child:

"I know your name, sweet mother — you are Louise Michel."

VI

Then one by one she pointed them out to him, there in the vast multitude grown vaster because
  of his presence.

All those whose words he had hurled as spurting bombs in the night,

All those of whose graves he had made his trenches, who had died like, him, by the ropes of the
  kings and the faggots of the priests and the stones of the blinded mobs;

And as she named them, they rose and smiled, and some raised up their right hand, and others
  bowed lowly and knightly, and others stood up at attention like soldiers, but most kissed
  their fingers to him.

"This is Watt, called the Tyler, who rushed through the gates of London, with the artisans and
  husbandmen of England, and made the king kneel before the villains. He was murdered
  like you, from behind.

This one, barefooted and ragged, is Masaniello, who assembled the councils of the rabble in the
  fishmarket of Naples, and made the holy emperor tremble, and the pope forget his curses
  and remember his prayers. He was murdered like you, from behind.

That hooded one there is Bruno, who sits between Prometheus and Lucifer, the third lighter of
  the unextinguishable fire, who blew out the candles of the temple that men might see the
  greater light of thought. He disappeared in his own incandescence, burned alive.

And this little man over here, with the blinking sore eyes, he saw farther than the course of the sun. He is Jean Paul Marat, the head surgeon of Liberty and friend of the people. He was stabbed in his heart, where his love dwelt.

And that is John Brown, who reproclaimed the Gospel of Jesus through the muzzle of his western rifle, saying that the freedom of the black man is the black powder, and so of the white man also. He was hanged.

And that is Francisco Ferrer, the brother of Socrates, who was shot for teaching the youth the secrets of the gods; and next to him Katoku, who was strangled in a dungeon, and Tolstoi, who announced the second advent and died of loneliness in the unpassable circle of glory . . ."

And many more she mentioned and pointed out to him — all, save the One with luminous face who sat in the middle of the clearing

Until, when her sweet task was done, she addressed them all and said: "Fathers and mothers, and ye brothers and sisters, comrades all, this is Karl Liebknecht, who stood up in the storm alone, and alone wrecked an empire of hate that a hundred armies could not break. Like all of us he was defeated in the end, but like all of us he died the death that is not extinction, and saved the Idea. He has come to us. Shall he stay with us? Shall he live?"

And all the Senate of the Dead stood up and thundered: "He shall live!"

VII

Then the One with the luminous face, after the acclaim was done, arose and stretched out his hands and spoke at last and said:

"For righteousness sake he was persecuted, and for it he died, and because of these things it shall be done to him as it was promised;

And great shall be his reward in the kingdom of heaven, which is life everlasting in the unextinguishable thought of mankind.

For he shall not be forgotten, and by the memory of the living he shall live eternally.

Yea, and all those who wait and believe shall never call him dead, for there he is only silent, having spoken his words, and he is only immobile there, having done all his tasks.

But when the day of resurrection comes upon the world, as it was foretold, and the day of the final deliverance,

He shall not be among the wise and the meek and the comforters who are invoked in the grey hour of anguish and doubt,

But he shall be rather among the heroes and the doers who are called out by the living in the bursting dawn of the dead, and he shall hear and answer with a shout from the heart of the storm:

'Here I am, my Comrades. I am not dead. I have been marching right along with you, by your side, towards the great source and the great estuary, and lo! ye saw me not!'"

By the Kremlin Wall

At the foot of this wall
Which for five centuries cast the shadow and the terror of the Cross
Over one hundred million men
Lies the Envoy of the First Republic to the First Commune.
He arrived here in the fullness of time
To see the fulfillment of the last pledge of Liberty,
And he bore witness of its truth even unto the silence of this earth.
He died of hunger and passion at the age of Jesus
And by this grave he recorded another of your glories,
O Youth! O Romance!

Here,
Through the hacking of four boards of red pine
And the digging of a seven-foot furrow,
The axe of Abraham Lincoln
Met at last the spade of Leo Tolstoi;
And by the eternal spark struck by their united steel
The Russian Soviet Republic
Forgave and blessed the Workers of America
Burying with her own Heroes,
John Reed.

On Lenin's Fiftieth Birthday

Victory, lightning-faced, flame-winged, has come
Just on the day it was told by your prophets and seers,
The harbingers of your great day, the builders of your highway,
The blazers of your world-trails!
Holah; ye the axmen of truth, blasters of lies and wrongs,
Torch-bearers of the sun, incendiaries, petroleurs,
Marshallers of the storms, thinkers and pioneers,
Hurlers of proclamations, bomb-throwers of song,
Raisers of mobs and altars, knights of the mad crusade,
Arise! Break from your chains, burst through your jails.
Tear though the noose of the gibbets — the day of days has come!
For lo! the Red Army has broken through the blockade,
And Russia that spoke with the Bible, now speaks though the cannonade

And her spokesmen that were in the dungeon are now on the barricade
In Berlin and Dublin and Rome!
    Gone are the days of despair,
    Come are the days of your glee;
    Debout les damnes de la terre!
    For Wilson rides a wheel chair
    And Trotsky has reached the Black Sea!
And now that Lenin is fifty and he can rest, as your law
Prescribes, and now that Brussiloff is crashing through to Warsaw,
Rest you also, Mother Russia, O full of glory and blood!
The rainbow is wreathing your head, your ark has conquered the flood,
The fates are fulfilled; your task is done. You have labored enough!
For gone is the pale little father, a little wind blew him off,
And the big father also is caught in the rifts of the gale,
The holy synod is filling with the red wine of the grail
And the white bread of the host the peasants' bags and the gourds;
Saint Peter and Paul is full of bishops and ladies and lords;
The hangman is kicking the wind, strung down from a minaret,
The children that begged for kopecks, now beg for a bayonet;
The ikons of the saints wear a red cap instead of the halo,
Grand dukes are in the mines and the miners in Tsarkoe Selo;
Kolchak, ripped in the belly is reeling and vomiting out
His guts and your gold, and Yudenich, like a boar stuck in the snout,
Is trailing his blood and his froth across the Esthonian lands,
And Denikin runs to his ships with his bowels in his hands;
The Letts and the Finns now own you have principles and fieldpieces
And you have four million soldiers to reclaim the Poles to Jesus,
Your teachers enlighten the people without any rest or stint,
And they give them one good rifle to explain every new book you print;
The workers now own everything, even their right to be born,
The peasants have taken in full, the flax and the wheat and the corn,
And in Moscow it is high noon, and in Europe it is the morn,
And the dawn is everywhere!
    Rest, then! Your dreams are all there!

THE LAST FRONTIER

On crossing the Russian border

Here where the old world died, the new began
Without a rule, a chart, a guide, a friend,
If this sign falls, here dies the last god — Man
If it stands straight, he lives world without end.
To set him free we were obliged to bend
His passions to his freedom, for we ran
Against all what he was for what he can
Become when both immortally shall blend.

But not into a spurious soft alloy
That tolerance stirs like a shapeless clay,
But like a hard grief welded with fierce joy
Upon the anvil beaten with the sledge
Into one serried broadsword that will stay
Forever rustless with a double edge.

TO MARIA SPIRIDONOVA

On her deliverance from prison

O thou who art so frail and pure and white
Like the primsnows that fecundate thy sod,
Thou who hast seen the shadowed cross of God
Bow past thy cell in thy remorseless night.

O man-sent Maid to conquer hell, o rod
Of burning steel that flowered into light,
Maria, thou shalt see the holiest sight
Since woman saw her first child in her blood.

Fierce sister sweet, open thine eyes and see!
Behold dispelling the auroral mists,
The pentecostal flame of Liberty!

Flung out like thy distress against the skies,
Beating thy dungeon with thy shouts and fists
And fanning the young sun — the red flag flies!

To Helen Keller

On a youthful picture of Helen Keller and her teacher
Ann Sullivan Macy framed with a laurel wreath.

Madonna from whose eyes the world's tears flow,
When I behold you with your goddess-child
Resting her head against your undefiled
Maternal breast, I turn mine eyes, and lo!

Along a flowered lane of Florence go
Beatrice and Laura, while among the tiled
Slim-pillared porticos, appeased and mild,
The sun-seared eyes of Alighieri glow.

I think then surely once this picture fell
From a cathedral vault while heaven bound
Flew up from it the babes of Raphael.

Till Benvenuto, seeking God's last grace,
Picked it and framed it with the wreath that bound
The lost head of the Nike of Samothrace.

To Eleonora Duse

Madonna you are old as the first tear
Of woe, you are as young as the last smile
Of hope, ever renascent like the wile
Of love, self-raising the deadly spear

Of hatred, seeress, mistress messenger
Of hate and pity, passion, deadly guile,
Behold the ghostly pageant, up the aisle
Marshalled and led by Aeschylus and Shakespeare.

In masks, in rags, in ermine and in stocks
Painted bewigged, the somni-eyed cortege
Stops at your feet by the footlights and asks

What is art's meaning, mistress of your age,
And you breathe back: Wait till the curtain drops
Then come and look upon the darkened stage.

For the Shakespeare Memorial Theatre

Stratford-on-Avon

Herein William Shakespeare for you and me
Reveals all of Life's lore that we may know it —
Above him is but God, but even He
Stoops down to listen to a greater poet.

March 1919

Holah! Awake! The horns, the drums
Are still, the war dogs crouch and snore,
But peace, the tyrants' harlot comes
Again atinseling with gore,
And from her ancient bag of tricks
Pulls out again the same foul hoard
The flag, the crown, the crucifix
The knout, the shackles and the sword.

Awake! The ancient beast lies dead
Upon the steep highways of time,
But from her carrion the winds spread

The foul pollutions of her crime,
For ten old men in Paris swore
And a hundred fools in Berne concurred
That all shall be as it was before
The same old law, the same old herd.

But on the world's dismantled roofs
Amidst their orgies break and blast
Agalloping on unshod hoofs
The chill alarums of the past,
And as the tocsin tolls outspread
And a thousand hosts advance unstemmed
Behold the Sabbath of the dead,
The ghostly pageant of the damned.

They come from France afar and near
They come with mightier offerings:
The dandy powdered Robespierre
To write new warrants for new kings,
Danton, who hurled two million men
Across the mountains and the sea
And dwarf Marat, from his rat pen,
The surgeon chief of liberty.

Look, on from Italy they press
The tribunes of the common herd,
The Gracchi and the Brutuses
The thought, the law, the axe, the sword,
And Masaniello, ragged, unshod
Who made the mob his justicer,
And Bruno, next to Lucifer,
The second enemy of God.

What if god-glutted England flap
The banner of the auctioneer?
Here bursts another thunderclap,
The second Runnymede is here,
And Watt the Tyler storms the gate
Of London town, and with his seers
And pikemen, Cromwell rides in state
To claim the king's head from his peers.

What if America, the first
To raise the red rag, comes the last?
Her soil untrod by kings, uncursed
By new-born gods, shall break the blast
Of the great trinity that come
Forevermore the red age down;
The fife, the banner and the drum,
Tom Payne and Crispus and John Brown.

Hail fools and justicers of fools!
Lord executioners of wrong,
Wherever else is silence rules
Your fierce example in the mob.
You were the thought, she is the faith,
You were the call, they are the strife —
Out of your glory that is death,
Here comes the glory that is life.

And lo, from all lands of the earth
Against the lie unveiled they call
The witness of your deeds that freedom
Shall ever grow and ever die,
And as the tocsin peels and tolls
They make their jury of your souls
And call for witnesses your deeds.

Hail fools and justicers of fools!
Hail prophets, seers and pioneers,
Come sit in silence
Come Lenin, Liebknecht, Markheim, Debs,
Haywood, Longuet, Serati, Wiers,
Come ye the lictors of the plebs,
The incendiaries and petroleurs,
Of all that's old, with the world's youth
Come with the weapon of our right,
With hope that's might, with faith that's truth
And love which is a plebiscite.

And as the mighty summons roll
Across the earth, let intercede
The thought for thought, the soul for soul
And against the deed call out the deed.

But if the dungeon and the noose
They set against the crying soul,
Against the gun let us unleash
The torch, the axe and the petrol.
The pogrom and the barricade,
The Saint Bartholomew of love,
And she who gave the accolade
The block, the axe and the lanterne,

And she who preens her first desire
For her great nuptials with the Right,
The chastest daughter of the fire,
Our Virgin Lady Dynamite,
And she whose lust was never fed
The grim, the fierce, the saturnine
The widow of ten thousand dead
Our Holy Sister Guillotine.

Come, vagrant pilgrims of the soul
And make the ramparts with your dead
Whatever must be said is said,
Whatever must lie low is still!

On the Death of Franz Joseph of Austria

One hundred times and one as dusk grew red
The cannon boomed. The belfries tolled and clanged,
Dogs howled, hallucinated men harangued,
Pale, babbling mobs; and as the rumor spread,

All lights went out and doors and windows banged,
While sixty millions sighed and cursed with dread:
"The wolf-faced carnifex of God is dead,
Dead is the Imperator of the hanged!"

Then sleep and love grew warmer in the down
Of Austrian beds, and all bowed with a sob
To death, save three who raged beside the tomb:

One was a harlot who has missed a crown,
One was the hangman who had lost his job,
And one a dreamer with a useless bomb.

END OF A PERFECT DAY

May Day 1920

Like a tomboy the evening now rides home
Across the cantering hillside through the leas.
Her cheeks all freckled by the gourmand bees
And her stubbed toes sucked purple by the loam.

She cast the fish-hook moon across the gloam
To catch the early stars above the trees,
And through her broken teeth into the seas
She squirts the hungry spittle of the foam.

From her pursed lips the wild winds promulgate
Unlawful tunes and kisses through her realm.
And when at last she sits down by her gate

She sees her ship come in with sails of gold,
With her young peasant captain at the helm
And seven howling kings chained in the hold.

THE PACIFIST

Ecce homo!
He has powdered and rouged his cheeks which were seared and cracked by the furies of the
    sun;
He has blued his piercing black eyes which had seen all the flaming nights of hell;
He has bleached and curled his bristling red hair which the hailstorms had beaten and
    disheveled;
He has trimmed and perfumed his savage beard which smelled with the smoke of combusted
    ages set afire by the shrapnel of his words;

He has rounded with placid siestas his lean flanks, and where his tunic of sackcloth flapped in
    the wind of the race, he has draped the toga of the tribune pleading for a repentant world;
He has filled his mouth, once bitter with the sands of the simoon, with the caramels of oily elo-
    quence and well-meaning quietudes;
And where he held the lash convulsed with febrile angers, behold now, my warrior brothers, the
    flowered twig of pudendal innocence and bloodless misericorde.
Is he the one who is to save us, and whom we are to rescue?
Or is it the other, the lighter of unextinguishable fires,
The shouter of incandescent words,
The buccinator of irresistible charges,
The petroleur, the blaster, the wielder of the axe and the bearer of the torch,
The vexillary of the blood-soaked labarum of the plebs?

Whom shall we demand for the guest of our revel, whom shall we claim for our toastmaster
    when the dawn comes,
My comrades, my mates, my warrior brothers, my lords and ladies-in-waiting of the scarlet
    queen?

* * *

Let the fat babbler die! Death to whom death is the goal!
The crown and the cross to him! the moat and the lime to him!
Hail to Barabbas! Give us Barabbas! We want Barabbas the bandit,
Him and his short-haired woman!

To Mussolini

A man may lose his soul for just one day
Of splendor and be still accounted wise,
Or he may waste his life in a disguise
Like kings and priests and jesters, and still may

Be saved and held a hero if the play
Is all he knew. But what of him who tries
With truth and fails, and then wins fame with lies?
How shall he know what history will say?

By this: No man is great who does not find
A poet who will hail him as he is
With an almighty song that will unbind

Through his exploits eternal silences.
Duce, where is your bard? In all mankind
The only poem you inspired is this.

To Franklin Delano Roosevelt

Franklin Delano Roosevelt,
By the inspired will of the people
And the solemn mandate of history
Four times the thirty-first President
Of the United States of America
Nothing can add to thy glory
But thou still addest to ours.

For thy clear vision into our future
We give thee the laurels of the seers,
Blessed be thine eyes.
For thy mighty valor in battle
We give thee the oak leaves of the heroes,
Blessed be thy great heart.
For thy belief in us and in our power
To set ourselves free from all fears
Aye even from the fear of death,
Blessed be thy faith.
And for the crucifixion of thy body
And the anguish of thy soul
We lay a garland of myrtle and cypress
Under the rainbow
Where thou sleepest immortally.

There will be
A greener and more fruitful earth
For the new world of men
Now that thou liest in it
Our master our father.

Italia Speaks

(A Monologue)

Almighty God of the universe and ye Gods of my lands and my seas, behold, what they have done with me!

Where are you now, Jupiter, Apollo, Minerva, Mars, Neptune, Lords of the Thunder and Lords of the Waters and the Mountains? See what they have made of me!

Where are you my sons? Where are you, Mutius, Camillus, Manlius, Marius, Julius, Scipio? Where are you Garibaldi? Look what they have done with me!

They have struck me between my eyes and on my breasts with spiked fists; they have weighted me down with chains, me, who was ever ready to set the whole world free!

I am reduced to rags and tatters and filthy shreds, I who had always worn the armor of the warrior, the mantle of the priest and the robe of the lawgiver!

Who has made of me a scullion to the vampire of Berlin, of me, of me, an empress, a goddess, a mother of mankind?

Who has made of me the Cinderella of Nations, the starveling waif of the world?

I was the parent of fruits and grains — my chariots dashed all over the earth, not to hurt or subdue, but to teach men how to tame horses and drive plows, how to crush olives and grapes into oil and wine, how to weave cloth and how to read and write and think.

I laid roads, I raised aqueducts, I builded cities throughout Europe, I won and gave out empires and gave the world the first universal language.

Three times I arose from the dead, I did it alone, by myself, though I never really died. But always poets and troubadours came from all parts of the world to sit at my feet and to rest their heads on my knees — singing my praise and my glory in all the tongues of man — and artists came to paint my face only to be dazzled and awed by its splendor and always ended by painting my feet. And to me came the first Apostole of Jesus and reared his Temple in Rome.

Only a little more than a century ago, came Goethe to weep over my hands his Roman elegies, then came Heine, then Byron, Shelley, Keats, Browning. God, how many! To sing of me and to me, and to die and be buried in my bosom like my own, my very own.

Then came my grandchildren from America — the singers from across the Ocean Sea — Whittier, who smote down slavery and Lowell who buried it, and Longfellow who came to kiss Dante's brow on a slab of cold marble . . .

Then, then my poor children went across the main in search of bread and honest toil, expecting new and greater sorrows, millions of them, millions of them and you, America, received and sheltered and fed them, and they were true to your motherliness and your pity.

And now, after compelling me to declare war on Greece, my mother, and France, my first born, the two monsters have compelled me to declare war against you, America, my youngest child, my fairest one!

Where are my other stalwart sons, the knights of the high seas, the challengers of the fog, the lightning and the gales? Where are you Christopher Columbus, Giovanni da Verazzano, Giovanni Caboto, Sebastiano Caboto, Amerigo Vespucci? Where are you, America, my daughter?

The twin ogres in black and brown have polluted my gardens and befouled my palaces and besmirched my triumphal arches and my monuments, but they cannot scar my face nor shame me.

I am the purest essence of the earth. They can bludgeon me but they cannot defile me. I am forever young because I am eternal and I am intarnishably beautiful, because I am Art and Poetry and Music and sunlight.

My daughter, America, come to my rescue! Stab the one assassin, the renegade, to the heart and cleave in twain the other assassin of the North with your mighty broadsword and let him fall into two shadows into the earth, one to the East and one to the West, forevermore, forevermore, world without end.

Battle Hymn of the New Italy

Freedom comes! Arise and greet her
Mine Italia fair and great!
From the wounded shrine of Peter
Where you crouch and weep and wait,
From your ruins your blood hallows,
From your desecrated graves,
From the dungeons, from the gallows
Rouse the legions of your slaves.

Toil-bound, bent with black disasters,
Hunger-mad to feed the Huns,
You gave mansions to your masters
And foul hovels to your sons;
Aye, through ages half forgotten
Ever wandering from your goal,
You the Empress God-begotten
To the Beast-born bowed your soul.

Rise, our Mother, in your regal
Armor and your shackles break!
Roars the Lion, screams the Eagle
Growls the Bear: O Italia, awake!
Where they hoisted noose and sabre,
Where the chains of shame they wrought,
Raise your hand, Italian Labor,
Lift your voice, Italian thought!

Rise and break into their revels
Flashing lightning from your eyes,
Hurl your hosts of famished devils
In their drunken paradise,
Till the outcast, till the lowly
Shall their bloody altars blast
And the damned shall be made holy
And the first shall be the last!

MALEBOLGE

Mulberry Street

Despots behold! The desolate houses lean,
Hell's innest barbicans, against the skies
Along the tortuous moat of this latreen.

The archangels that rebelled against your wise
Commandments are here tortured in this pit,
As you may hear from their discordant cries.

The damned are these who sinned against your writ,
The wayward who in their wild errant modes
Did all the things for which you were unfit.

Piling above the clouds your white abodes,
Plowing the earth for you, filling your marts
And burrowing through your subterranean roads.

Hark now unto the creaking of their carts,
The calls of ear-ringed bawlers, and the sturdy
Whistles of your policeman who imparts

Your penalties to them; list to their wordy
Quarrels and bargains, and above the din
The plaint of the sad-throated hurdy-gurdy.

Smell the foul wind of woe that blows within
Their cells, whence even the daylight recoils
At the polluting stenches of their sin.

The fetid garlic of the brew that boils
Between the sunfire and the stove beneath,
The vats where fume the sweats of unclean toils.

The crusty lips of babes that gasp for breath
Torment them so, that tho' be great their guilt,
So bitter is their doom that less is death.

Mulberry Street is this. The domes they built
Are not here, Despot! Here is where they mold
And shall decay until their last seed wilt.

Pursuing their mad dreams through ways untold,
They spread through all your lands and all your seas,
Eating black bread and lavishing bright gold.

Peddling their dreams, their songs and fantasies
And quickening with the fevers of their blood
The pulse of your ferocious industries.

All that they made they never thought it good.
All that they loved, they never could revere,
All that they wished they never understood.

Slothful and sleepless, lustful and austere,
Gloried by death, made deathless by rebirth,
The progeny of Rome, Despot, rots here!

Yet pity not, for here dwell faith and mirth,
And to the future still they reach their hand
That thrice led forth mankind and held the earth.

Their house of bondage is within their land
Of promise — but their haven they'll attain
When blares the clarion of the last command.

If they pay now in full with shame and pain
The price for having shunned your monstrous feast,
Tomorrow they shall rise and win again;

For they who gave the most and asked the least,
But dwelled in royal state in every sense
Of their fierce flesh, are of all men the freest.

And if they seek nor praise nor recompense
'Tis that they have all things in their grim lot;
The memory of an old magnificence,

The pride of earth-old glories unforgot,
A strength unsapped, a dream inviolate,
The power to see beauty where 'tis not.

The magic of the lyre that softens fate,
For their new love a flower and a song,
And a stiletto for their ancient hate.

And lo! out of this evil maw erelong,
Born of their indestructible desire
And nurtured with the bitter milk of wrong,

Passing invulnerate through flood and fire,
Shaking the sloth of ages, they'll convoy
The chariot of the Hound who from this mire

Will lift them to their heritage of joy.
He will heal all their wounds and blot their scars,
And with red tongues of wrath he will destroy

You, Despot, and the trophies of your wars,
And lift the young Republic's head above
The diadem of her reconquered stars!

For though she closed her door to them and drove
With chains of want and scorn their august clan,
She still remains the daughter of their love.

Aye and of all the names the lips of man
Have uttered since the day they set to roam
And their long quest for the free land began

On which to build at last their gateless home,
America, no word of glowing fame,
Nor even the eternal name of Rome

Beats faster in their bosom than Thy name.

A Meeting at Astoria Hall

That Friday afternoon the hall was full of Italians who after four months of lockout had met
again for the twentieth time to listen to the same exhortation — "Be stronger now that
you are poorer for strength is the handmaid of right and injustice is the stepdaughter of
poverty."

The hall was too crowded with Italians to hold anything save memories of wars and victories
and the lilting alarms of new clarions and the fierce echoes of anthems — when they came
in.

They came in from nowhere, like the thunder, like death, like the presentiment of a senseless
joy, like the wild urge to sing — twenty-seven old men in long black robes came in.

And the noisy assembly heaved up in a great wave and roared and reared like a mad charge of
horsemen, and fell back like a broken billow leaving the front seats twisted and bare like
a gnarled shore full of rocks and wreckage.

The hall chairman leaped up to me on the platform and panted — "There must be a mistake but
it is too late to straighten things out. These are the old Jewish tailors who were discharged

first before the lockout. You know the story — 'We are businessmen not a charitable institution — we can't have pensioners in our shops.' But the Amalgamated will not let them down, we'll fight for them. Better say a few words in English even if they do not understand everything. Please!"

Quietly, one by one, the patriarchs filed in and walked up the aisle and sat in line in front of the platform with their skull caps that looked like a row of sacred lamps and their white beards that looked like a placid flock of sheep browsing in the sunset.

Then they became very still and an ancient holiness fell over the hall, and all cigars went out and all other heads became bare and the warlike tumult of Italy was quelled once more by the assembled people of Jesus.

And then I who had come with a message of defiance and scorn for everything that was not new and young and impudent, I was suddenly taken back to the years of my boyhood when I was told to honor age next to the memory of the great dead and to hail its crocked staff in the marching pageant of the people before the lilies of the virgins, the joys of the poets, the trophies of the warriors and the garlands of the athletes.

And lo! the multitude disappeared before my eyes and I only saw them, the elders of our new state.

And so I forgot the cruel siege, the cries for food and help, the dread anguish of the dying day that was bringing the stillness of the Sabbath over an ageless woe, and spoke only to them who sat in silence, without stirring, without approving or disagreeing.

And I thought that they, the eternal fugitives from persecution and servitude, had been toiling at all the true labors of life for six thousand years, that three times they had circled the earth always leaving for new hopeless pilgrimages.

Yea, and I realized with a pang in my heart that none of them had achieved anything save the knowledge of numberless calvaries and the iron will to go up their pathways, and two silver candlesticks and an old book that reshaped the world and their God's promise of an everlasting Sabbath of rest at the end of their journey.

And these men who were as old as human toil and human sorrow had been cast out of the house of Mammon, first.

So I spoke and I spoke with my mouth and my eyes and my fisted hands, with whatever clamors and aches in the depth of me, and I was not conscious of anything but the dull feeling that I might be hanged for the things I was saying.

Then a mighty roar leaped up from the hall and a dazzling light beat upon the swaying white beards and reverberated in the dim walls and I retreated to my silence, but they still sat serene and inviolate.

And behold! They were no longer the beggar at the gate, the wailers by the ramparts of Babylon, the pleaders for life and mercy.

For they will be sitting at their high noon in the front stalls of the first and ultimate senate of Mankind when the great dawn breaks and mantles the world!

CREDO

I believe in the Empyrean, eternal and limitless, but empty and useless if it were not a carpet and a stool for the feet of Man and a pillow for his thought.

I believe above all things in the beauty and grandeur of life which is not all ours but is a trust assigned us and which we must return on time with usury, always with many tears and occasionally with all our blood.

I believe in Love, the only antagonist of sorrow, the only one who defies, engages and hurls back, even if it does not conquer, the great Enemy.

I believe in my Neighbor, my Brother and my Friend, who, however poor and humble and dishonored and voiceless he may be, is always better than I, and to him I reconsecrate each day my travail and my faith so that we may march together towards the goal of the great dream beyond the portals of the unknown.

I believe in the goodness of Man, of all men, even those who are called brutal, mean and cruel, for they also suffer by making their kindred suffer, for pain is the father of goodness, which throbs and cries however deformed and imponderable it may be, even in the heart of the assassin.

I believe that Evil — hate, jealousy, greed, cowardice and war — is not a part of the immutable destiny of man, but is a resultant of obscure forces that he can and will destroy when the sunshine of fraternity will clear his eyes and kiss and smooth his brow, the coffer of his invincible thought.

I believe in Art, imprint, signature and seal of Man upon the architraves of the earth, magnet of all the arms raised from the abysm, and in thee, foremost of the Seven Sisters, Poesy, first cry and last breath, laughter and rattle, mistress and teacher of all human ecstasies.

And I believe in thee, Science, who, having put your hand into the hand of your elder brother Labor, descend and delve into the deeps, and scale and lower the altitudes, without fear, tireless impavid, sleepless, unfillable like the cradle, insatiable like the grave.

I believe in Liberty, breath of the Universe, light of the Stars, illimitable and irreducible for she has no kingdoms nor castes, nor schools, nor ancestors, nor heirs, neither beginning nor end, even as time which only the fool attempts to measure.

And I believe in Justice her handmaiden, who levels her highways and who stands first by the right of my Brother and then by my duty, and is of both the peace.

And I believe in the Tomorrow, infallible and imperishable of which Today is only the fore-thought, even as the night is for the dawn, the Tomorrow limpid and young, the athlete bathed by the fury of the hurricanes and dried by the typhoons, crowned with laurels, erect against the fates and the infinitude.

And I believe in Thee also, Oh Lord, whoever Thou art, wherever Thou art, whatever Thy name, Oh Love, Oh Truth, Oh Father and Mother of all, not only because Thou seest above and beyond my mortal eyes, but because I also need in my pride and pain to bend and kneel before a Supreme Pity that will illumine, even if it does not explain to me, the terrible mystery of Life.

THE NUPTIALS OF DEATH

Whose shoes are never seen
but whose carriage
is always heard rumbling
boisterously outside.

One morning, long ago, death came to see me,
Death came to visit me, like a widow who comes to cry out her woes, and one cannot very well put her out.
She came shuffling her pantoffles of silent felt, wet, soaking-rotten with the mires of cruel roads;
I heard her shuffling them on the floor outside, cautiously,
Like a fat and lazy landlady who is used to the sudden silences of brothels —
Her feet lapped the floor like the tongues of dogs that lap the blood of slaughterhouses.
I heard her cough outside the door, quietly, feebly with discretion, as a compunct undertaker does before he comes in, to announce without words to the weeping ones that it is time to take down the corpse . . .

That is I thought so, for I knew that she was coming

But perhaps she did not cough and the shuffling I heard was that of the leaves of the book I was reading.

Then she knocked sweetly on the door, timidly, with great dignity, a knock of refinement, a well mannered knock as prescribed by a solemn etiquette,

For death is a decayed grand dame.

She is an impoverished gentlewoman

Who, when she knocks on the doors of life

To solicit a loan or a promise,

Is dignified and grave and pudibond

As a grand duchess wrapped in an antique mantilla of black

Over a venerable crinoline of some other color.

I did not open the door, nor I said "Come in" (for I never open the door to them who knock not hard and boisterously and do not fume and fuss and swear and grow impatient as my friends do, and my mistress and my enemies and the police) but I lifted up my eyes from the book and I looked.

I looked and saw a mouse run away to his hole

I saw under the interstice

The toes of my Lady Death

Wriggle like the keys of a piano-player

Treading along a gouty minuet

In the backroom of a bankrupt saloon.

Suddenly, while I raised myself on my pillow

And dropped on the floor the Holy Bible that I was reading

To get out of it the winning number of a lottery.

Death loomed up before me, cauled in her hood,

Wrapped up in her tawdry kimono

And decolletéed in her night chemise

Like a cocotte

Who is going to see a show, or perhaps she is not.

For Death dresses no longer in black

And does not garble herself in grey

And wears no longer mourning like an orphan or a widow

And carries no longer the scythe and the broom of the witches.

But a smart little parasol,

And she harlequins the red and the blue

And the yellow and the violet

And all the other colors of the rainbow,

For what peculiar reason, I do not know.

She drew near to my bed very slow

And bowed, courteously smiling

And nodded, neither meek nor bold.

And I drew hastily under the coverlet, quick
Hot with the flush of shame, and did not dare
To look into her face, for I was not sick
Nor was I amorous-bent (being just noon)
To receive in my bedroom any lady.
But she bowed sweetly and drew near and said
With even voice, quite unabashed and steady
As any worldly nurse would say: "Excuse me, sir,
If I disturb your sweet repose, but I have come
I am here on a very presing errand — My name is Death."
I kept quiet for a while, then I grew witty
And bold and answered: "Make yourself at home,
Please don't be bashful, I am Giovannitti."
And thus having done with the etiquette
Of courtly presentation, I grew bold
And looked at her. And she was fair and good to look upon,
And even a bit of a piquant coquette,
And did not look more than thirty years old.
But she was white, so white and colorless
That suddenly my tepid bed grew cold
As if a wind had blown the coverlet
And the hoar frost of March fell flat on me.
But the sweet visitor smiled wide and free
Out of the rainbow of her strange array
And spoke with a hoarse voice, as if she were enrhumed
By my own sudden chill, in this strange way:
"All through the million million years I go
Avisiting the world and men, no one
Has spoken to me as you have spoken now.
That speaks most well of you, I must avow.
But tell me, why
All others have chased me out
As if I were a foul and stenchy beast?
They all have turned from me in wrath and hate?
Still, the Maiden am I immaculate,
The empress of the world,
The most thought of, the least to be forgot,
The most desired and the least understood.
Still I am fair and good
And yet who knows of my unspoken love?
Aye, many seek me out,
Tho' most avoid me,

But none has sought me out for my own sake,
As one desires a woman coveted,
As all desire life for life's own sake,
And not for what she gives.
If one ever invoked me,
It was for what my help would bring, of course,
To kill remembrance, to allay remorse,
To pass beyond to dark and nothingness,
But never a wiseman, never a great seer,
And not a poet, nor hero who shunned
Life ever sought death for the sake of death
Not for what lies beyond.
I have been like a great wide-open door
That people cross to enter and come out
To go and never to return about,
To heaven, and peace, oblivion and to fame.
But who upon the threshold where he came
Has thought of me alone, of what I am,
Of me alone as the great definite goal,
Just for the love of me to be sought for,
In the flesh in the vision, in the soul?
Ah Poet, I am I, I am not peace,
I am not sleep, I am not rest, nor anything, nor any less nor more
Than was in the end and the beginning
Just Death. I am all things for I alone
Am I, the thing itself. Come then to me!
Love me, take me. Great is my embrace.
Only in this great hour I live. Dare!
Be bold! Ravish me! Rape me and I shall be your slave."
Into her great red eyes I drove my stare,
Wrapped in the virgin lust of her white glare
My body rose and fell, eager, unsteady
I stretched my hands, already sweetly dead
To all save her appeal — and then I said:
Frightened, all-weak, all-strong,
I stretched my hands to her and pleaded: "Lady,
Grant me first an immortal song!"

She smiled then to me and she answered
As she bent lower on my pillow
So I could see the sweet furrow
Between her breasts and the greed

Of lips and teeth in her throat:
"What is a song when a deed
Eternal, O Poet is near us?
I shall make you fulfill all the mandates
Of all the gods,
I shall make you the despot of heroes,
I shall make you defeat all the powers,
Conquer the worlds and the hours
And rise again after the fates;
If you will ask me nothing save the joy of the dead
And take me into your bed
Just for the fire that devours
Your flesh may be quenched in my snows.
Violate me with all your senses,
Like the master does to his slave,
With all the madness of lust
You could not appease in your life,
Not for your pleasure, but mine,
For I am still the untouched wife,
The Queen, that has killed all her lovers
And all her husbands before
The threshold of her bridal door.
Poet, thy great hour is come;
Take me, you alone shall rest between my arms,
You alone shall cool your face between my breasts,
You alone shall bite and hurt with your teeth my frosty flesh;
And by the incantation of this sweet deed,
And everlasting hour of love that's dead,
You shall give up your dreams, in your last breath
But you shall find yourself and conquer death,
If death alone for what death is you crave."

So spoke to me Death, all dressed in reds
And yellows and blues and greens, and purples, ablaze
With all the sun's cleft rays
By her falchion and all the crazy flags of the world.
And I looked at her; I alone dared look at the pearled
Sheen of her face, without any dread nor hope,
Without having called her, without having put her out
In my bedroom that the morning whitened and blued.
And lo! while my blood fermented and brewed
By the breath of the cold-hot words

And the kisses that sizzled and baked
Stirred by her tongue on her lips
She flung away all her veils,
And in the glows of the whitest of all the white lusts
She stood there, all-glorious, all-naked,
And the snow of her flesh made even the sunlight eclipse,
White and immaculate like the snow and
The queen of all the red fires and all the white frosts.
And I stretched my arms to her, shaking and mad
In the spasms of her passion divine,
And she stretched her own and she hurled
Herself on my chest, and supine
She lay under me till the eve
And we both forgot life and the world.
And from that day I have forgotten how to suffer.
And I have learned how to die,
And I keep on dying all the time.

MOUNTAINS

Sometimes, when I look up to you,

And the skies on your head,

To your unchangeable snow

To their immobile cold blue,

I think of the valley below

Where little things move and grow

Unendingly.

You seem then to me

Like stricken pitiful wights

Knocked down by the blows of the heights

Weeping mad torrents of tears

Into the river's cold bed,

Foolishly counting the years

In the jail of eternity.

Sometimes when I look up to you,

I think of the dead.

Atavism

My mother's sires were men of solemn looks,
Long-haired, bewigged, lace-collared and rapiered,
Who served the king, obeyed the pope and feared
Nothing, save God and books.

My father's folks were of the common sap,
Poachers and court physicians, and such breed,
Who had nothing but princely veins to bleed
And royal game to trap.

And thus, entangled in such strange discords,
In strange contrasts my twofold nature raves,
And now it loves to kick and flog the slaves,
And now to hang their lords.

Mea Culpa

The man am I who wakes all night to mark
The coming of the dawn; and lest it creep
Past his closed eyes, he listens for the sheep
To bleat, the cock to crow, the dog to bark;

And then, ere the upswing of the lark
His vigil wearies and he falls asleep,
Nor does he waken till the sun is steep
Into the noon, and all his soul is dark.

Then, tho' his hope is lost and gone his task,
Still he must rise and walk into the drawn,
Mute day, nor knows he whither, nor dares ask
What power impels him, nor the reason why,
Save that love stayed when all passed with the dawn,
Lord, even like that foolish man am I.

"DIXI ET SALVAVI ANIMAM MEAM"

Son, a few years from now I shall be dead
Leaving nothing behind save a short laugh
Without an echo, and an epitaph
Hewn on a shapeless stone above my head,

On which the best for me that can be said
Will be: Here lies a man who oft did quaff
Red wine to mock the fools and the riff-raff
Who almost drowned him in the blood they shed.

He did not fight when war was all men's toast,
He did not die when death the whole world swept,
He lived when life was useless if not thrown

Away. He did no thing but dream and boast,
But when Russia arose he sang and wept
And thereby saved his soul and won this stone.

ALL FIGHTERS' DAY

O you, who stand grim and ready in the sudden eclipse of your day,
You with the rudderless heart, lovers and rovers of storms,
Whose torch is the lightning, whose goal is the lair of the spent hurricanes,
Lend ear to us, listen and answer, for ours alone is this day and we teem with all the tomorrows.
We know you will not be disturbed if broken and fierce and obscure and without peace is our
    message,

For your lips also are hardened with sneers and battle calls,
And your blood that has not been infected with the sacred vaccine of the lamb
Shall foam now like a strong must in the raised goblets of spring,
To warm the old heart of the earth and redden the cheeks of the gods.

My Friend, I and my comrades, Men and She-Men, have elected you
To the magnificent feast of this last baptism of War,
And today you will be initiated in this mad brotherhood of ours
If you but ask to come in by striking your sword on the door.
Whatever the host you are serving, whatever the name of your cause,
If nobler your flag seems to you when nearer you see the red death
Of those whom the rabble call fools, and men and history call heroes,
Then you are even as we, and surely one day we shall meet
And clasp our gauntleted hands on the main highway of life.

May you then, with or against us, know all the furies and struggles
Of the spirit that never weakens, of the flesh that never wearies,

And all the pains and the woes and the blows and the wounds of the world
And hunger and thirst and cold that make the body twin to the earth.
May you see on the lips of your bride the same anguished smile that first chained our destiny
    to that of our warrior women,
And the cowardly fear of your shadow on the brow of your best trusted friend,
And the tears of your mother, the mightiest army to rout,
And the black stare of your children, the thickest wall to break through;
And your own loneliness of him who leads and can never turn back,
Nor stop, nor ask anyone for the road to the summit,
The only place where is rest.

Let the long hours of waiting come to you, and the endless aeons of desire;
And let yourself know hope when hope is less easy than despair,
And despair when its bludgeons strike harder than the hammers of faith.
And may you also, brave Friend (cruel or craven is he who denies this)
In those collected hours when return to you the silent messengers of your heart that have tar-
    ried behind your lusts and the dust of your feet,
May you also know the tears that are neither sorrow nor weeping,
Nor regret or remorse, nor any backwash of the past,
But the pillaged trophies of your soul that has surrendered nothing in the red sunset of defeat,
Nor has gained aught in the chilly dawn of conquest
Save a sharp stone to sit on and a view of the battle-scarred field!

Strange friend, whoever you are, gregarious or solitary,
Preserver of antique lores or wrecker of ancient wrongs,
Or assertor of earth-born rights, or confessor of new-found truths,
If you receive this message and return it even as it came,
You shall not have the peace of the peaceful nor the happiness of the happy,
But you shall have Force and with Force you shall be nearer to Wisdom,
And you shall find your true comrade, your guide and your servant — Yourself,
And feel no longer alone.

And lo! you shall eat black bread and bitter olives with the ancient hunger of the athletes,
And you shall drink the rain of the storms and the water of the cataracts with the magnificent
    thirst of the Titans;
And you shall sleep on the bare earth, watched by the fires of volcanoes, the ample sleep of the
    Cyclops;
And in your sleep you shall walk with the gods, and in your waking hours you shall discourse
    with the sages and converse with the heroes;
And you shall have whole and unsullied the body and the soul of your woman, or your man,
    forever beyond the fear of death or new desire;
And your children shall grow around you nimble and swift and hard like the colts and the
    wolflings,
And you shall be unafraid of the heights and of the deeps, like the eagle and the shark, being of
    uneatable flesh.
Aye, and men shall lay traps and nets for you and you will not live long nor placidly,
Even unto the end which comes alike to a sun and to a worm.
And what imports the most, my friend, you will not die in bed amidst flickering tapers and odors
    of sanctity, and cries and wailings and lamentations and benedictions.

But your spirit, ravished in the arms of the tempest, shall be extolled in the triumphal paean of
    the wind, above the ramparts of time, unto the glory of the unbeholdable light!

MISERERE

Though I still remain where I always stayed,
Half hailed, half mocked, half understood
My sword now raised when once I prayed
In vain for peace and brotherhood;

And though I still hold undismayed
My ship against both crown and rood,

My task cannot be much delayed,
Dear life, if I must still make good.

Before the dull years overwhelm
My spirit, give me one sure omen
That I'm still fit to steer the helm;

Before I break down pass my strong
Faith to my son or to my woman,
Or grant me but one deathless song.

The Death of Flavio Venanzi

To Onorio Ruotolo

Being a faithful narrative of the death of Flavio Venanzi:
to keep his memory ever green in the hearts of all rebels good and true,
and for the glory and the remembrance of the noblest of all May Days — MCMXX.

Onorio, I have been waiting for the brown swallows that fly close to the earth and never rest and never sing and no one knows whence they come and whither they go, save you and I and another, my sweet friend. But now that they have come with the fanfares of the June sun, I shall speak of Him, for the speaking of Him will be as goodly as the sight of fresh grass around the rusted tools of our grief.

For though my wind-swept home is ready once more for all the beloved visitors, and though there is still wine on my table and new books on my shelves and a new-born man-child is in my bed, and though my wife is full of milk and tearful dreams, I know that I must speak of Death, Onorio, lest my life which has grown empty of songs become also deaf to their echoes, and yours, which is piling rocks wrathily, grow unmindful of the chasm you dig.

He died one month ago, on a rainy afternoon when his home was darker because of the absence of the sun and of his children, and because his mother and his wife and his brother and I were there and knew not what to say. Alas! and another silence was there also, the silence, sullen and disconsolate of his books, the dull taciturnity of a youth wasted in the search after truth which is in the cadence of a marching multitude, and happiness which is the unison of a working song.

The Doctor, a fine strong man — his name was Alfred Raabe, who became acquainted with him when he could scarcely know anyone, and who grew to love him in seven days, and wept and came to his funeral — said that it was pneumonia. But I, his comrade and friend, and you

Onorio and you Salvatore and you John, know that it was the Russian blockade that killed him, and so it should be recorded in the red register of the People, among the finders of new roads.

Do you remember? When Yudenich was tearing like a boar toward Petrograd, he would stand flame-eyed like a blazing candelabrum before the map on the wall repeating slowly and lowly and with a strange twitching smile; "Stop him, Holy Mother Russia, stop him! I believe, I believe!" And though he wanted it to appear that he was mocking the priest chanting a liturgy, we knew that it was the love that passeth all understanding that was burning his soul even to the incandescence of adoration.

Do you remember? When news came that Kolchak had been cut to pieces and the possessed of Denikin had been driven into the sea like a herd of swine, he seemed to grow taller and thinner and whiter as he said with a quiet voice: "I knew it, I also have helped with millions of others who believed with them and fasted and watched and kept awake with them till it was done." And though we teased him for his mystic fervor and he also laughed merrily with us, still we knew that an ancient truth had been revealed once more and made almighty.

And then, when the Apotheosis was near and half of the world was singing the paean with upraised arms and the other half was trembling with joined hands before the fires of the divine aurora, the ululations of the jackals rose again in the receding night, the Poles marched forth with spiked boots on the flower beds under the rainbow, dragging back the gibbet of the Czar behind the cannon of the Republic. On that day his wrists grew weary with the long upholding of the bowl of his blood; on that day his passion and his agony began.

Poor Flavio! He was meant to be a watchman by the beacon, a signaller in the night, not a shouter of fierce alarms. He had not been born with clenched fists, he had not been nursed with milk and blood from a wounded breast, he had not been schooled in the stabbing with heavy swords. His flesh was not weak — it was his spirit which was too eager and tyrannous. And so he died of too much believing, of too much wanting of himself, he died without even the sullen solace of revenge, without even smiting a politician on his purple jowls or spitting back the gall and the vinegar on the fat hairless hands of a bishop.

Ah, Justice of the New Day, write this down also on the crowded page of your wrath!

II

It is not easy, my comrades, to write of our lost Brother. He was one of those who should rather be sculptured with the true nail of the Cross out of a white ecstasy, facing Gene Debs, as Luca della Robbia carved the meeting of the two starving saints out of an April cloud charmed by the Umbrian wind into stone. But if the words are needed, being the mainstay of the life of Man, then he should be better remembered by his friend Musso reading to us and to his children the second canto of the *Inferno* in a soft twilight without shadows.

For Flavio also was tall and lean and a bit bent in the shoulders through a long contemplation of the deeps and the little things of the earth, ants and men and wiggling wisdoms; and he also was sharp-nosed like Dante, whom he knew well and with whom he had been discoursing every night intimately and pleasantly as they visited each other — about the bitter bread of exile and the ingratitude of the People and the barrenness of revenge save through the unappealable sentence of a song.

He was white of skin, having been cheated of experience, which is a searing noonlight, in the pursuit of thought, which is a dweller of the gloaming. He was frail as a whispered word and as light as a seed, but like these he carried with him upheavals and everlastingness. For he had been born in Rome, where all things are made for the eternities, and like a Roman he had wasted nothing that was not burned to the gods or scattered before the chariots of the heroes.

He was not of many words, having spoken long with himself before stern judges; he was a quiet arguer with his own anger, the youngest child of his heart trained with mature wisdom, but he was a quick yielder to the weakness of others — ready to forgive passion, implacable against the spirit. And he came very near to the portals of glory, for he could sing other men's songs with the same rapture and the same torture the gods have assigned to their spokesmen and their revealers.

He enjoyed wine only because of the hand that poured it and was wise with food like a tree that draws it honestly out of the communal stores of the earth; and he was wary of the seasons like a migratory bird forever in search of sunshine. He loved the People and had known no sufferings save theirs and for their sake and if the People were supreme he should now be walking along the aisles of a cheering multitude to the rostrum of the lawgiver.

He honored his father and his mother and had sold all his goods for the poor; he had never borne false witness against his neighbor or his enemy nor coveted anything save to be forever more than himself in the service of the workers; and he loved only one woman and she blossomed faithfully and beautifully by his side; and he had two children strong and fair and after the inner likeness of himself — and the name of the girl, was Alba, the dawn, and the name of the boy was Elios, the sun, and he was only thirty-eight years old — a long, long way from the Dusk!

III

When they sent for me, he had been asking for me for hours. It was before sunrise and I walked on slowly, thinking that thereby I might delay the unjust sun. I jeered at the absurdity of his wanting to see me on such a morning, when the clear hours and the dark ones had been encircling us like a myrtle fence, impassably. They told me that his heart was growing weak, but why? He had not strained it with strenuous athletics; it had withstood the hunger of many sieges; it was still armored with the heavy mail of faith; it was still guarded by the outer breastworks of love.

And why should he die save that he was poor? And why should he be poor save that Poverty is the mother of Freedom? Ah! his poverty was the achievement of a hard task, the supreme conquest of the Soul, and he loved it and hugged it tight to his heart, warming it with gentle words, the humble words of the olden days when to be poor was next to being holy, when none who was not hungry and cold and barefooted could enjoy the companionship of the bearers of eternal tidings and gain the freedom of rest.

When I came to his home he was already delirious, seeing wondrous and terrible things. His Mother met me at the door, dry-eyed and embraced me and said "My son, it will be very hard for you, for this is the first time he hurts you. But you must be strong, like me, his mother." Then the other Woman, whose face was like a Nimbus in the dark, completed the unspoken request: "The children are asleep." And our strengths became one, and I did not cry and they grew invincible, for women are afraid of nothing, Onorio, save of men's tears.

At first I did not see him, for every light was lost within and without me save the last desperate trust in the clemency of time; but when I saw him and shook hands with him in the dark, fiercely, hoping to hurt him for the sake of my own strength, all the immortal words I had heard him say and read rushed to my lips and choked me. But I was brave, having been wounded, and I said: "Flavio, you must rally. We must fight till the end. Think of our Russian Brothers."

He leaped up on his bed; he sat straight, he raised his hands in a noble gesture (Oh the beauty of his long hands raised above the heads of the People!); he became transfigured, almost invisible in the glowing ardor of his Faith, like a flame in a strong sunlight, and answered with his resonant voice: "Certainly, Arturo, and I am ready. We must fight till the end for the Social Republic." Then the Doctor and the nurse pushed me gently to the door.

But as I was going out I turned my head again—and there he was with his face lifted to the vision of immortal things, conversing placidly and learnedly with One who was sitting quietly by his bedside — about Russia and the Workers and Tomorrow and the glory of Death when she ministers unto Life. And I know that on that empty chair turned askew between his moist pillow and the rain-chattering window, holding fast to his fevered pale hands, sat our smiling Brother, Lenin.

IV

For seven long hours we watched him, his mother and his wife and his brother and I, while the children were away. For seven long hours we fought gainst the madness of tears, avoiding each other's eyes, talking of futile things, dreading the intrusion of visitors and the open window and the door ajar and the stealthy steps of the nurse who moved ghostily about. And we all felt stronger because of the dismal distraction of the rain and I felt thankful, Onorio, that you were not there.

Then as the afternoon wore on a sort of evil impatience with hope came over me, and I grew resentful of realities and returned meandering through the labyrinths of old, peopled with the wraiths of other men who had believed and tried and failed. And so the spell of the Dead came upon me as soothing as a lullaby, and I pulled out a book from the shelves and opened it and read silently to the soul of the Woman who was walking on by the soul of the Man.

Onorio, there were many books on the shelves, old and new and terrible and meek and loud and soft-spoken, the round horizon of a lofty belvedere mighty like a gathered multitude. But the book I picked at random was the "Little Flowers" of Saint Francis, and the page I opened was the Canticle of the Sun, the first poem written in our gentle tongue:

> "Blessed be Thou, O Lord, for Brother Fire who is strong and robust and full of valor!
> Blessed be Thou, O Lord, for Sister Water who is chaste and cool and gracious!
> Blessed be Thou, for our Sister, Mother Earth!
> Blessed be Thou, O Lord, for our corporeal Sister Death!"

And lo! at that moment the Nurse came in slowly, her head down mourning the lifelong failure of Man, announcing without words the Mighty Visitress. And there She was, the sweet Sister of our Body, the Lonely One, the Silent One, the Sleepless One, the Liege-Mistress of all our endeavors, the Completer of all our tasks, the One forever shunned and misunderstood. There She was on the threshold tall and pale and august and full of grace reminding us with bowed head and outstretched empty hands that they honor Her the best and they know Her the most who receive Her like an illustrious guest only with the simple words of welcome and the unwilling tears of pride. Then with Her entered into the room the Evening and the Children, weeping.

V

On the morning of May Day we drove the body of *Flavio Venanzi* through the East Side, and many men and many women walked behind the hearse in silence, though all the voices of Springtime and Mankind were pealing mightily in their hearts an ancient psalm of anger and deliverance. We walked for ten minutes and we passed six mounted police patrols with guns and cudgels and heavy frowns, and thus did the turbid world of the non-living pay its last homage of fear and hatred to the sweet Tribune that was dead.

Then after we pilgrimed after Him to the goal of all things, save the songs of love and labor that resurge forever after the swift sleep of the night, we burned Him in the Crematory of Long Island, without speeches, without chants, without tears. And so what had been a living thought shriveled and died down to a handful of ashes in the fist of the Monster that writhed and gloated in the shadows.

But somewhere in the vast hall, towering above a heap of wild flowers, shone terrible and splendid the Sign of the Resurrection — the Scythe and the Hammer made into a cross over a round field of red carnations. And above in the damp heavens of May Day there still lingered the smell of the Easter Lilies, and pulsed and shook and roared and trembled the echoes of the Workers' and Peasants' wrath in a rising hosannah of thundering guns, blasting across the quaking Earth a swifter roadway to the Sun.

And there was a great rejoicing among the damned and a fierce tugging at the chains.

To the English Language

Athlete, builder of towers, digger of chasms,
O navigator of all the great seas, escaltor of all the heights,
I have put my hands in your hands to grapple with you,
And I have understood you, your strength and your anger,
You the deed that has become word.

O abandoned foundling of a thousand orgies of men and gods
Picked up night after night upon all the doorsteps of the earth,
Beggar and burglar, law giver and pirate, lavisher of gifts, hoarder of booties,
Raw, rugged, unharmonic, miserly collector of music,
Unloved worshipper of all the graces,
You shriek, you moan, you growl, you rustle, you roar,
Aye, and you sing, too, but you are unhappy,
For you cannot weep and be holy.
Bestial like all flesh arut and in pain, all-enveloping like the fog,
All-hiding like the clouds,
All-stirring like the wind,
You are neither of the earth nor of the skies, but just thyself, unknowable and lonely like death.
How would I love you, O Fierce One, were you not so untiring and cruel and so grasping and
    selfish a denier of truth!
But I admire you in awe and I acclaim you;
For you and I are strangers, but we meet often,
You and I are enemies, but we have a habit of truces
And often feast and get drunk together, at the same table with the flesh of the same quarry from
    the gourd of the same song.
Like two rival hunters after the chase.

Scientist

You have said Amen to all unexpected truths: You have broken through and brought down the arches of the eternal incantations of Nature, giving names and features and scopes and actions to their dismembered debris, making equal in the distinction of their separate lineage the spine of a steel wheel to the framework of the Universe; the dregs of a chemical precipitate to the astral coze of the Milky Way; the pollen of the edelweiss on the brow of Mount Blanc to the dandruff on the gown of the Lord Chief Justice.

Aye, and of a monkey you made man.

Love

You say I love you no more,
And I answer that I don't know what love is, now that all is war.
But I am happy when you sleep peacefully by my side
And the touch of your warm flesh on mine always wakes me up,
And when the rhythm of your breath is heavier, when you lie on your heart
I cannot fall asleep till you rest quietly with your face towards me.
And when I wake in the morning and see that you are there
I am happy and glad of the new day, and stronger because of you and the light.
This is more than love, because I don't have to tell you alone,
And I can write it down and let people read it
Without feeling ashamed or ridiculous.
And make some of them even feel that I am revealing a new truth
And writing a poem.

The Old Tree

The old tree by the old tenement yonder
Is the only horizon I see from my work-window.
Its foliage brushes against a window on the top floor,
Whose shutters are always closed
So that the old tree is not even a screen or a blind.
I know that no one ever loved it, that is why I love it
And loving it I feel in myself something that hungers,
Something that was lonely in me since the day I was born.
Firm, stalwart, serene old tree, unhurried, unproud,
No longer growing, nor yet aware of its end,
It never bore a fruit in its long faithful life,
It never shaded anything that was not its own shroud,
It only lived for the wind that passes and never comes back,
Useless, barren, flowerless, without any purpose
Like this thought and these words.

Seven Saplings

Seven saplings in a crooked row,
Hop along, skip along the first blades of grass,
A winter may freeze and a summer may glow,
A war may come and a peace may go,
But these things always shall come to pass:
A king will have a crown and a queen,
But he will never be sure of his head,
A rich man will never be too lean,
Workers will never be overfed,
Race horses will browse in pastures green
Until the ragpicker picks up a song
That fell from a garret and a poet's tongue
And takes it to the scissor grinders
And they make it sparkle and make it splutter
And they throw it up from the dirt of the gutter.

The Closed Window

Again after so many years I passed it by near Grant's Tomb,
And its shutters are still closed tight, and they are no longer green.
Ah, that the rain and the sun that turn all windows abloom should be so cruel to this, and leave
    it so drab and mean!
What does it mourn in the dark, what is inside the blind room
What lies wide-eyed and immobile wrapped in the folds of the gloom,
Decayed and dreadful and lewd?
An old love, an old faith, an old dread of the great towers that chime
Before this dead hermitage to the swirl of the multitude?
What is hid there? The bright trappings of soldiers of olden times,
Or the veil of brides now oldened to a barren decrepitude?
Unheeded love letters, blood-tainted records of glories or crimes,
Or just the frills and the toys of long-gone maidens and lads,
Or belated inventions, ruins of deeds unaccomplished,
Poems that were never read, writs of great wisdoms demolished
By the sudden surge of new fads?
Perhaps the cult of a failure, perhaps of a masterpiece,
A misery that dreads the light, a triumph that woos the peace
Of an ever even twilight.

Whatever there is in that room, I would love to sleep there tonight.

You Sing No Longer

You sing no longer now at your machine
As you mend faded rags and faded days,
Nor do you seek the sunlit spot between

Your flowerless sill and my unfilled bookcase.
You sew and sigh, and as you snap the thread
You seem to fear to break the wonted ways

Of our joined thoughts. And yet love is not dead.
Nor any of its pledges is defiled,
For we still sleep together in one bed

And in six months we'll have another child.

Words Without Song

O distances, rival sisters of the altitudes!
I who have given up floating on the mists towards the stars
That I might follow the tracks of trains and the hoofs of horsemen,
Shall I forever stay here in the Bronx?
Shall I never see the red linen sails gliding through the amaranth of the Bosphorus?
Shall I never plant a young sapling by an Indian pagoda
Or beat with my sweaty hands the silences of the Sahara waiting for a human echo?
Shall I never curry a colt at dawn in the plains of the Pampas
Or turn my back on the minarets of Moscow and follow the wind and say:
This sun is going back to whence I came?
Shall I be forever immobile in the Bronx saying to the tailors and the dressmakers
The glory of man is on the picket line downtown?
And the end of life is two hundred dollars a week?

The Death of a Billionaire

He died as he had lived, the papers said.
But so do most of us who, being dead
To every joy of life save in the giving
Of all ourselves, and though dead go on living.

But he who bade us work and procreate
And starve and kill and live, being so great
He was not cursed to live. When all his measure
Was full, he sought in Death another pleasure.

He sought the rest that he denied his kin,
The peace of mind and calm that was not in
His aims nor our dumb tasks; a friend, a neighbor
Was death to him, — to us another labor.

To us another burden which was meant
To dig his grave, to build his monument
To praise his name, to write and read his story
To toil for his estate and for his glory.

So we shall raise his statues in the squares,
Hospitals, parks, clubs, ships and thoroughfares
Will bear his name; on every arch and portal
It will be graven — but is it immortal?

Living, he thought it so; and if hope leads
Even the dead, and if he still can read
His name on bronze and stone that no time can dismember,
He'll think that glory reads and will remember.

And thus he feels assured that the great task
Of life is to secure a double mask
One, hard and cruel, to enrich one's being
The other, mild and soft, for the sight-seeing.

Two masks in one, reversible to show
One face the life, one face its afterglow
One to sell men, machines, souls and petroleum
The other to sell God in his mausoleum.

For who shall lay a hand upon the dome
Whereon he rests? The column of Vendome
Still stands rebuilt on its eternal stamen
As Titus's arch is and that of Tut-ankh-Amen.

But glory stalking stealthily and solemn
Beyond the tomb, the tablet and the column,
Will read but one more name, and will not know it
For glory is not a tourist but a poet.

As They Go By

As they march up the boulevard even the elm trees are alert and stark like sentinels,
While the taps of the drums fly like hunting falcons in the sweet air
And all is still, save their feet and their hearts and our hearts and the sullen sun,
And the listless road that leaps forth to the mad goal.
They are marching perhaps to death, all of them,
And I shall not accompany them with anguish and joy and thrills of songs and auguries of
        battle,
For I have walked much further and nothing of mine shall reach them,
Save this yearning that they come back alive to the place whence I started,
Or reach me wounded and starved on the way that I may heal and feed them.
And yet . . . and yet ———

Ah not to kill my unknown brothers, not to destroy
What I could never rebuild,
Not to take what I could not give back, not to shout impious unforgivable words,
Not for the dumb subservience to the beast ambushed in me, as in them,
Not even for the hate of the wrong, nor even for the love of the just ———

But for the glory of going unafraid towards the ultimate night,
And the pride of leaving all behind for the nothingness that is ahead,
For the touch of steel against steel, a supreme meeting of souls,
For the weighing of my worth in the scales of other eyes, without hope of appeal,
And for the revelation of my inner effigy in the cruel mirror of death,
And for the knowledge that my life is not worth more than any other life, nor less;
Aye, for this alone I would march up with them as they go where all spent passions go
And hail you with upraised hands at the turn of the aimless road,
O War!

THE UNKNOWN SOLDIER IN WESTMINSTER ABBEY

The shades stalked from the great sarcophagi at midnight
And crowed around the quiet youth.
"What have you done that you are here so young and so soon?"
"I worked at a loom," he replied, "since the age of nine,
Weaving cheap muslin and calico for the dress and the shrouds of the poor.
Five hundred yards a day for five shillings a week,
And had no other ambition save to weave a thousand yards sometime
And get ten shillings.
One day, as I held the quivering hand of a girl
They told me to go and be a hero.
For they said glory for a man who wove calico
Was only in the dying
For the safety of our great land,
Lest men who made calico and gingham and muslin
Be paid seven marks a week instead of seven shillings.

"I died of a British bullet fired into my head by my captain
One morning as I stood and shivered and raised my hands in joy
When from the other trench a voice cried:
'Peace, brothers, peace! Hoch die Internazionale!'"

THE SECOND ARK

Disease — the flesh is still corruptible and mean —
And age, and its master death.
We have gone and gone and gone, and we come back to the same things —
But we came back all together brothers and we shall be forever together
This is the law,
This is the glory of this day.

This we have won: that one day we called upon us a great flood
And we built ourselves a great Ark as big as our ancient land
And we got our entire race into it, and all the birds and all the beasts and all the good things
And none perished save the few who would not come in when we called them.
This we have won: that we made a great deluge of all our desires to find new things and new roads
And we bade all men come in, all ideas, all religions to find out where we should go, what we
should do,

And this we did — for we know now that we are going nowhere save where we always stood
And we must do nothing save what we always did,
That we were foolish to believe there was any hereafter
Nor any new happiness save that of being together.
For this let us bless the flood that has taught us the truth of labor.
It was said of old, in another day of great trial that the poor shall always be with us.
Yes, truly forever. But now we shall all be poor together, and poverty will lose its terrors, being
     so to all men, like death.
We shall not covet riches, there being no rich men to envy.
Patience and poverty are the shepherds of all of us: we shall not want.

GLORY

For the seventieth time in two weeks
I passed by a bronze statue in Washington Square.
I don't know who it is. I never read the name.
What did he do? Who was he?
I shall never read his works in the public library,
Nor look him up in the Encyclopedia
Tho' I pass the statue for the millionth time.
Or perhaps I know all about him,
Except that some fat Tammany Mayor
Put him up here as an argument for re-election.

On the bench under the pedestal I saw last night two lovers kiss
In the hurry of time, in the hurry of youth,
Before, Death, the last roundsman comes to shout "All out."

Love of men, love of women, love of seizable things,
Forgive this perishable thought.
I am full of wasting blazes,
I am hollow with brittle caresses.
I shall never congeal into a bronze — I am liquid.
I would rather be a worm wriggling for a day
Amidst the toes of a beloved carrion
Than be this statue for a millennium.

LAST LOVE

And though I have not found any surcease
Of this wild pain, and though I am still glad
Of love and its deceipts, I am grown mad
Of its warfare that shows no signs of peace.

Grant me, then, life, one token of release
In my pursuit of calm: give me one bad
Or one good woman, new or such I had
And lost, a wife, a concubine, a niece

Of Satan or a daughter of the Lord —
Anyone save the one who would enmesh
My soul and hold and own it by one word;

A woman who will fill my arms and mug
With everything I ask from wine and flesh
And then sleep still beside me like my dog.

"LA BELLE DAME SANS MERCI"

Often, my lady, have I been distressed
Seeing behind your head my shadow pass,
Until I saw a phantom casque of brass
Where I had placed the halo of the blest.

Then on your heart where heroes found no rest
Nor children sleep nor I my dream, Alas!
I felt the hidden scales of the cuirass
Press deep into your amazonian breast.

And yet, though no celestial mantle shroud
Your limbs, nor mystic light your eyes expand,
Beneath your feet I see a rising cloud

When I, an infidel become a priest,
Raise to my lips the chalice of your hand
And kiss upon its palm my eucharist.

JOHN REED

What difference does it make
Whether a few bricks have fallen off the Coliseum
Or another bolt has chipped the brow of the Jungfrau?
What difference does it make whether you are alive or dead,
So long as you stand like these, Jack?

Yesterday we were drinking wine together
Cracking nuts with our teeth,
You and Bill Chatoff and Bob Minor and Max and Bill Haywood and I;
Today — or is it tonight? — you are playing cards
And testing the edge of newly forged blades
With Benvenuto
And Cyrano
And Salvator Rosa,
While Francois Villon fills the glasses wishing hard that you would ask him to read his new bal-
    lade,
La Ballade des Copains du Beau Temps Jadis.

You are all right, Jack, wherever you are, with such a steady and goodly company,
And we are gladder and stronger because you went away
And you did it so splendidly.

There will be hardier seeds and mightier metals in the soil of Russia,

Now that you are there.

MOSCOW 1921

A rift of clouds and wings around each sentried steeple
Red flags licking like flames the gold of the great dome,
Silence and sunlight and the bared heads of the people . . .
The Red Army is coming home.

SONG AT EVENTIDE

Life, everything I dared ask
You promised and bade me to wait,
But none of your gifts you completed.
Lest I grow now too conceited
By failures and charge them to fate,
Life, let me finish one task.

Not one that will prove any truth,
Nor one that my lusts will assuage,
But one of patience and valor:
Out of the sulking and squalor
Of this recalcitrant age,
Life, set me free from my youth.

Let each depart as a friend
Who, the day after a feast,
Resumes a hard lonely journey,
Or as — after fighting a tourney —
Two knights both unhorsed and appeased
Clasp hands and pledge faith to the end
Blot not the scars that I hold
From this fair fight on my brow,
Make me not whimper or grumble;
If I have ever been humble
Before, do not make me so now,
Life, give me pride to grow old.

Not slowly, and yet not too fast,
But just as the law of the years
Decrees and the yield of the season,
With no abasement nor treason
To time, unconquered by fears,
Unprodded by hopes to the last.

Let me not be as a tree
Which though it bear no more fruits
Still casts its shade by your temple,
But make of it an example
To saplings: stripped down to the roots,
Reset it a mast on the sea.

Let me be as in the time
Of summer a river sucked dry
By the fierce suns on the mountains,
That to the springs and the fountains
Does not conceal or decry
Its reeky bed and its slime.

Let me be as in mid-June
A self-destroying hail storm
Which, having spent its last thunder,
Leaves to the West Wind the wonder
Of rainbows, and clouds, and the warm
Sunset and the dawn of the moon.

Let me not woo you again,
Life, with bought wiles and false looks,
Make not of your poet a showman;
Henceforth let me have but one woman
About me, and children and books
And joy in the deeds of new men.

TIME'S END

To my martyred Brother, Carlo Tresca,
who dreamed thus with me.

Thus shall it be. When after this long night
The Rebel Fiend at last clasps hands with God,
And his black wings become great fans of light;

When the last tyrant has been slain and trod
Into the loam with the last cursing priest,
And every liar lies in his foul blood —

Judge, soldier, legislator, journalist —
Life shall then burst into a gale of fire
And cleanse Man from the taint of saint and beast.

Beauty rewed at last to man's desire
Will make all laws her handmaids and will strip
Them naked of all weapons and attire

Like lovers and athletes. Strong hands will grip
Soft hands in freedom's pact and there will rise
New orders with the rule of brethrenship.

Then will the meek stand girt with boundless ties
Of strength, and strength will boast a humbler name,
Then power will be a servant in disguise,

And pride will be the better side of shame;
Then art and thought will take the place of strife
And only toil will wear the wreath of fame.

Thus shall it be. For should this prove less rife
A reaping of the gifts you promised me,
You whom I worshiped as the breath of life,

Had been its foulest curse, O Poetry!

"TRE DONNE INTERNO ALL COR MI SON VENUTE" — DANTE

Three women came about my heart
As I leaped forth to live, to dare;
One gave me opulence, one art,
One taught me never to despair.

The first was she whose vast empires
A lustless flash of love unrolled,
The chastest flame of all my fires,
My unseduced sweetheart, Revolt.

The second one brought me no thing
Though she was dowered regally,
But when I wept she bade me sing,
My barren mistress, Poetry.

Then she, the third, who linked her name
Forever to my fruitless life,
The only claimant to my fame,
My lady Death, my pregnant wife.

A Chronology of
Arturo Giovannitti's Life

1884   Born on January 7, in Ripabottoni, a small hilltown in the province of Molise in Italy.

1900   Completes *liceo* (high school) and emigrates to Canada, where he studies in a Protestant seminary associated with McGill University in Montréal.

1904   Emigrates to the United States, settling in New York City, where he studies briefly at Columbia University.

1906   Collaborates with Carlo Tresca on the socialist journal, *La plebe*, and begins renouncing his early religious beliefs.

1908   Joins the Federazione Socialista Italiana (Italian Socialist Federation). His first poem (in Italian) appears in print in the May Day edition of *Il proletario*, the Italian-language newspaper of the Industrial Workers of the World (IWW).

1909   Moving from being a reformist socialist to revolutionary syndicalism, he starts an Italian-language radical journal, *La rivista rossa*. He still participates as a member of *Il proletario*'s editorial committee.

1911   Assumes editorship of *Il proletario*. Begins writing in English — his first article, against Italy's designs on Libya, was published in the *International Socialist Review*.

1912   Along with IWW organizer Joseph Ettor, he travels to Lawrence, Massachusetts, to help striking textile workers. Anna LoPizzo, a striker, was killed in a violent confrontation with the state militia. Even though Ettor and Giovannitti were miles away when the shooting occurred, they were arrested for inciting to murder, in part because the state authorities targeted them because they were active and effective in organizing the workers. While awaiting trial, Giovannitti writes "The Walker." Both are eventually found innocent by a jury.

1913   Steps down as editor of *Il proletario* but continues to write for the newspaper. Participates in the failed Paterson, New Jersey, silk strike. Writes regularly in English, especially for *The Masses*.

1914   Translates Emile Pouget's *Sabotage* into English for the IWW, and translates Leopold Kampf's drama *On the Eve* into English. His first book of English poems, *Arrows in the Gale*, is published with an introduction by Helen Keller. Establishes *Il fuoco*, an anti-war journal.

1915	*Il fuoco* ceases publishing and Giovannitti starts another journal, *Vita*.
1916	His drama *Tenebre rosse* is staged — one of many plays he wrote during his life. Both his brothers fought and died during World War I, serving in the Italian Army.
1923	Organized the Anti-Fascist Association of North America and became its secretary-general.
1924–25	Edited the Italian-language journal, *Il veltro*. In 1925, Giovannitti reunites with Joseph Ettor to lobby for the release of Sacco and Vanzetti.
1930s	Gradually stopped writing for the American press and centered on his leftist activities. His heavy drinking starts affecting his health.
1938	Publication of *Parole e sangue*, a book of his Italian-language poems.
1940s/50s	Giovannitti's health continues to decline. He eventually ceases all writing and political activity.
1957	*Quando canto il gallo*, a collection of his Italian-language poems is published in Chicago.
1959	Dies in the Bronx on January 31. He was separated from his wife Carrie and survived by a son, Len, and two daughters, Roma and Vera.

Notes

"Proem" — *buccina* is Italian for a Roman trumpet.

"The Prisoner's Bench" — Joe refers to Joseph Ettor.

"When the Cock Crows" — Frank Little was a labor organizer who was taken forcibly from his boarding house in Butte, Montana, and was lynched from a railroad trestle on August 1, 1917. Parsons, Engle, Fischer and Spies were executed for conspiracy to commit murder for the 1886 Haymarket bombing. Wrongly accused of the murder of Mary Phagan, Leo Frank was lynched on August 17, 1915.

"The Senate of the Dead" — Son of Wilhelm Liebknecht, founder of the Social Democratic Party of Germany, Karl Liebknecht took part in the Spartakist Rising along with Rosa Luxemburg in Berlin. The German Army crushed the rebellion and Liebknecht was executed without a trial on January 15, 1919. During the Paris Commune in 1871, a group of Communards lead by the artist Gustave Courbet tore down the Column Vendome, which commemorated Napoléon's victory at Austerlitz. Louise Michel was an organizer and participant in the Paris Commune of 1871. Watt Tyler led the Peasants Revolt of 1381 in London, demanding an end to the Poll Tax. Masaniello, an abbreviation of Tommaso Aniello, was an Amalfi fisherman who lead the revolt against Spanish rule in Naples in 1647. Francisco Ferrer Guardia was a theoretical anarchist and the founder of La Escuela Moderna in Barcelona in 1901.

"On Lenin's Fiftieth Birthday" — Work on the palace and park in Tsarkoe Selo (Tsarskoye Selo) was started in the early eighth century. Known in Russian as the "Tsar's village," the Great (Catherine) Palace served as the summer residence of the Russian emperors prior to the 1917 Revolution. Aleksandr Vailiyevich Kolchak was appointed an admiral in the Russian navy by Tsar Nicholas II; Brussiloff was a general in the tsar's army. Nikolai Yudenich was a successful commander of the tsar's on the Caucasian front. During the Revolution, his White Army forces were defeated in Estonia. Anton Denikin also fought the Bolsheviks unsuccessfully.

"To Maria Spiridonova" — Maria Spiridonova, a member of the Russian Socialist Revolutionary Party, assassinated Police Inspector Luzhenovsky in January 1906. Luzhenovsky had repressed the peasant uprising of 1905. She was sent to Siberia for that murder. On her release she blew up Chita Prison in March 1917. A member of the Left Socialist Revolutionary Party, she supported the October Revolution. In July 1918, she led an anti-Bolshevik rising. She was captured and sent back to Siberia and was shot in 1941.

"March 1919" — Bill Haywood, a prominent socialist, was a founder of the Industrial Workers of the World. He emigrated to Russia in 1921 and died there seven years later. Charles Longuet was a French journalist. He married Karl Marx's eldest daughter, Jenny. He was a member of the Paris Commune of 1871 and editor of its official newspaper.

"The Death of Flavio Venanzi" — Known as the "Rodin of Little Italy," the sculptor, critic, editor, poet, illustrator, cartoonist and teacher, Onorio Ruotolo created a series of realistic plaster busts of immigrants and destitute tenement dwellers in New York City. Along with Giovannitti, he co-founded the short-lived progressive cultural magazine *Il fuoco* in 1914 but it soon folded because the two could not agree about Italy's entry into World War I. After 1930 Ruotolo disavowed his earlier political beliefs.

"John Reed" — Robert Minor was a radical cartoonist who supported socialist causes and women's rights. He later joined the American Communist Party. Max Eastman was a radical journalist who later renounced his political beliefs and worked in support of McCarthyism in the 1950s. Salvator Rosa was a seventeenth-century Neapolitan painter who also wrote a number of satires that were published posthumously.

"Time's End" — Carlo Tresca was secretary of the Italian Socialist Federation of North America and a member of the Industrial Workers of the World. He participated in coal miner strikes in Pennsylvania as well as industrial disputes in Lawrence, Mass., and Paterson, New Jersey. Leader of the Anti-Fascist Alliance, he was mysteriously assassinated in New York City in 1943.

AFTERWORD

*An arrow moves one way, the mind another. True, when the mind
exercises caution and when it is proceeds on a line of inquiry
it goes straight, not wavering, to its target.*
— *Marcus Aurelius*, MEDITATIONS

This volume comprises the collected poems that Arturo Giovannitti wrote in English. First published in different format and organization by E. Clemente in 1962 and then reissued in 1975 by Arno Press, Giovannitti's work bears witness to an important era — both culturally and politically. Giovannitti's extremely long and loose Whitmanesque lines, as well as his eulogy "The Death of Flavio Venanzi," "The Bankrupt's Suicide" and "Scientist," provide a key piece in understanding the development of the prose poem in the United States. Around the same time Giovannitti was writing these works, T. S. Eliot and Ezra Pound dabbled with their very short-lived prose poem experiments. Sherwood Anderson was also elaborating on Whitman's prosaic lines and natural speech cadences. And Gertrude Stein was gathering a fusion of poetry and prose into something the world had not quite seen before.

Giovannitti made prominent, but largely forgotten, contributions to American arts and letters during the first part of the twentieth century, well before Italian-Americans were recognized as making valid contributions to the cultural life of the United States — at least outside the realm of theatrical performers, singers and musicians. This cultural amnesia may be due in part to Giovannitti's radicalism and pacifism, in part to him not exactly living as a choir boy throughout his life and in part due to his reluctance to promote himself as a writer. Giovannitti, I suspect, would not have wanted to portray himself as a poetic innovator nor would he have wanted to write sophisticated, intellectual poetry. His mission was to sing to those slaving away in factories and sweatshops, to sing to those who (if they were lucky) could read his poems in various socialist newspapers and journals (but who were more likely to have had someone read Giovannitti's work to them or possibly heard him speak at a union meeting or political gathering). Giovannitti's political mission shaped his poetic vision and expression. As orator, agitator, organizer, poet, playwright, essayist, journalist, doubter and believer, he sought to better the plight of the worker. It is ironic that what Giovannitti strove for in the first part of the twentieth century has been steadily eroded in the latter part of that century and that this erosion has gained momentum in the twenty-first century. There has been a collective clouding of our cultural and political memory that life was better before government intervened in the interests of *all* its citizens. Giovannitti helps remind us that life was not better then and that we should not repeat the same mistakes that contributed to so much misery around the world. Now the message being preached is that whatever is good for the owner and producer is good for the worker and consumer — something that would not be unfamiliar to Giovannitti's ears. The common person owes a debt to Giovannitti and his compatriots for the battles they waged for the social and political gains that everyone takes for granted today. Let us keep Giovannitti's words in currency, let us listen to history and let us remember.

— GIAN LOMBARDO

quale [kwa-lay]: *Eng.* n 1. A property (such as hardness) considered apart from things that have that property. 2. A property that is experienced as distinct from any source it may have in a physical object. *Ital.* pron.a. 1. Which, what. 2. Who. 3. Some. 4. As, just as.